Twayne's Theatrical Arts Series

Warren French
EDITOR

Peter Watkins

Peter Watkins directing *The War Game*.

Peter Watkins

JOSEPH A. GOMEZ

Wayne State University

BOSTON

Twayne Publishers

1979

Peter Watkins

is first published in 1979 by Twayne Publishers,
A Division of G. K. Hall & Co.

Copyright © 1979 by G. K. Hall & Co.

Printed on permanent / durable acid-free paper and bound
in the United States of America

First Printing, November 1979

172460

Library of Congress Cataloging in Publication Data

Gomez, Joseph A
Peter Watkins.

(Twayne's theatrical arts series)
Bibliography: p. 199 - 203
Filmography: p. 204 - 10
Includes index.
1. Watkins, Peter.
PN1998.A3W3524   791.43 9233 0924   79-12947
ISBN 0-8057-9267-8

Contents

About the Author

JOSEPH A. GOMEZ was born in Albany, New York, on November 15, 1942, and was raised on "B" Westerns of the 1940s and 1950s. During his teenage years, he spent much of his time socializing in movie theaters. All of this changed in 1959 when he accidentally wandered into a screening of Tony Richardson's *Look Back in Anger*. From that point on, he became a serious viewer of films. He earned a B.A. in English from the State University of New York in Albany and his M.A. and Ph.D. in English from the University of Rochester. He has taught English courses at Temple University and filmmaking and film aesthetics courses at Mohawk Valley Community College. Currently, he is an associate professor at Wayne State University, where he teaches film courses in the English Department. Gomez is the author of *Ken Russell: The Adaptor as Creator* (Frederick Muller Ltd. and Pergamon Press). He has also written articles for *Film Quarterly, Literature / Film Quarterly, The Velvet Light Trap, Film Heritage, Film Criticism, Movie Maker*, and *The Journal of Popular Film*.

Editor's Foreword

ONE OF THE foremost aims of this series has been to provide an adequate appreciation of the unique work of Peter Watkins, who is unquestionably the least understood, most neglected, and most unjustly maligned artistic genius of this generation. As Joseph Gomez points out at the end of this survey of Watkins' remarkable accomplishments, even in view of obstacles that would have discouraged all but the most persistent visionary, Watkins has been the "conscience" of the 1960s and 1970s as George Orwell was of the 1930s and 1940s; but our contemporaries have been no more willing than people have been ever before to listen to their conscience instead of responding to hysterical drives toward material gain and mindless conformity.

Watkins' trouble has been that he has *not* been a "rebel"—a partisan propagandist pandering some Utopian program. As Gomez observes, the reply of a young poet in *Punishment Park* to an unfriendly question about the commitment of his poetry—"It's not committed to the revolution; it's committed to sanity"—might be Watkins' own motto. His work, therefore, annoys reductivists from both ends of the political spectrum—those John Steinbeck called "the lumpen right" and "the ecclesiastical left"—from textbook Communist reviewers to establishment bureaucrats terrified of "frightening" a childish public that prefers to pretend problems don't exist.

Indeed, the principal reason for suppressing Watkins' visionary works has not been that they would inspire rebellion and violence, "panic in the streets," but that they might drive insecure people to despair and suicide, depriving their paternalistic exploiters—like the church and state officials in *Privi-*

lege–of undiscriminating consumers of whatever trash is currently fashionable.

As Gomez suggests in passing in his analysis of *The Gladiators*, perhaps the best parallel to Peter Watkins is William Blake (1757-1827), the British poet who produced extraordinarily original and universally unappreciated works during an earlier period of violence and despair. Like Blake, Gomez points out, "Watkins does not want to be enslaved by another man's system. Instead of a reformer, he is much closer to being a political visionary in his rejection of current political movements, in his insistence on denying the postulates on which systems depend, in his striving for the decentralization of all structures, and in his affirmation of the dignity and worth of individuals."

Blake and Watkins were also remarkably alike in seeking to address the world through a unique combination of words and pictures. Blake preferred to present his "songs" and "prophecies" through engraved books which he prepared himself, using striking drawings (remarkably foreshadowing the work of Edvard Munch that Watkins much admires) not simply to "illustrate" a text but as an essential part of it. Watkins has sought, as Gomez shows in detail, to create in his work the same kind of fusion of images and sounds that will present a wholly integrated realistic reproduction of a prophetic vision.

Like Watkins, Blake was not at all understood. As Geoffrey Keynes points out in *William Blake: Poet, Printer, Prophet*, "a commemorative handbook" issued in 1964 in conjunction with an international exhibition of Blake's illuminated books, after Blake worked fourteen years on his last great prophetic poem, *Jerusalem*, "his message was not understood and the contortions of both text and designs were regarded as signs of insanity" (charges also commonly leveled at Munch if not openly at Watkins). Only five complete copies of *Jerusalem* are known, and Blake actually completed only one of these by magnificently coloring the illustrations. As he wrote to a friend a few months before he died, "It is not likely I shall get a customer" for the one book; and, in fact, he did not.

However appalling these parallels between the men, they offer some signs of hope for the future. Though Blake was ignored, despised, and left to die in poverty by his contem-

poraries, his obscure and "mad" illustrated prophecies are a
century and a half after his death among the most admired and
respected of poems in English, the object of reverent study by
many of our most distinguished critics. Such honor is small
comfort to today's beleaguered creator; but the prophet must
accept the traditional risk of being little honored in his own
land and time.

Technological advances in the very media that Watkins has
so imaginatively utilized at the same time that he has so
greatly distrusted their masters could be working to his advantage. The greatest problem Watkins has always faced has been
getting his works before an alive and appreciative audience.
His difficulties have been with nervous middlemen—theatrical and television administrators afraid of audience reactions
to works of undeviating integrity, and formalist critics who
have deplored his humanitarian concerns. (He has faced the
same kind of hostility from aesthetic zombies as the sur-
realists, with whom his work has affinities.) His pictures have,
therefore, rarely been shown on commercial theatrical or television screens, and major distributing organizations have
shunned them.

Since much of Watkins' work—rooted more strongly than
any other contemporary's in the tradition of amateur, experimental filmmaking—has been made in 16mm and especially
for television use, the growing availability of home videotape
viewers can make it easily available to small, concerned audiences. Even Blake's work commands no mass audience today;
and it is unlikely that austere, demanding, and uncompromis-
ing as Watkins' has been, it will ever, either. The challenge is
not to break down the resistance of mass distributors, but to
get around them—something that the high cost of film production and projection materials has hitherto made difficult.

Whether Watkins' work will benefit from these new de-
velopments depends, of course, upon the energetic efforts of
enthusiasts in discovering an audience for it; and such enthusiasts will develop only when they can find out what there
is to be enthusiastic about. As Gomez points out, Watkins has
been especially shamefully overlooked by taste-making film
historians. Hopefully, discerning studies like this one that try
to make us *see* what Watkins' vision has to offer will help get
the word around. We are proud to feature Peter Watkins prom-

inently in our evolving history of creative contributions to the cinema.

W. F.

Acknowledgments

THIS BOOK could not have been written without the assistance of Peter Watkins and Andrea Gomez. Peter Watkins not only provided me with numerous opportunities to screen his work and to meet with people who assisted him in making his films, but he trusted me with copies of his personal correspondence and spent countless hours answering my many questions. Although he cooperated in every possible way, Watkins at no time placed restrictions on me or attempted to alter any of my responses to his work. To say merely that Andrea Gomez provided support, advice, insight, and perceptive analysis would be inadequate. Her contribution to this book approaches collaboration.

I would also like to thank James Welsh, who was instrumental in the publication of this book and who is presently working with me on reference guides to Peter Watkins and Nicolas Roeg; Anthony Ambrogio, Anca Vlasopolos, and James Mullen, who read my manuscript and offered both encouragement and valuable criticism; Scott MacDonald, who discussed various aspects of Watkins' films with me; John Baxter, who sent me research information; Jacqueline Kavanaugh of the BBC Written Archives, who provided research material on *Culloden* and *The War Game*; Lillian Hinson, who typed part of the manuscript; and Warren French, my editor, who worked with attention, skill, and efficiency.

I am indebted to the State University of New York, Mohawk Valley Community College, and Wayne State University for summer fellowships which allowed me to conduct research and to secure key interviews in England, Norway, Denmark, and Sweden. The following individuals graciously gave of their valuable time and allowed me to interview them about

Watkins' work: Stan and Phil Mercer, Dick Bush, Odd Geir Saether, Jeff McBride, Poul Martinsen, Pål Hougen, Ada Skolmen, Grethe Hejer, Nicholas Gosling, Lars Löfgren, Richard Cawston, Derek Ware, Egon Blank, Richard Weber, Bo Melander, Paco Härleman, Gunnel Nilsson, Peter Suschitzky, and Florence Bodin.

Translations of material in French were provided by Anca Vlasopolos; Swedish translations were done by Richard Weber, and Danish translations were made by Jeff McBride. Acknowledgments for photographs contained in the book are as follows: Peter Watkins for *Diary of an Unknown Soldier, Dust Fever,* and *Punishment Park,* Tony Rose for *The Forgotten Faces,* John Baxter for *The War Game* and *The Gladiators,* Paco Härleman for *The Trap,* Odd Geir Saether and New Yorker Films for *Edvard Munch,* Steen Herdel for *Evening Land,* Helge Jensen for *The 70s People,* the British Film Institute for *Culloden* and *Privilege,* and John Salerno for the photo of Watkins on tour.

Finally, early versions of sections from chapters 1 and 4 appeared in *Film Quarterly, Film Criticism,* and *Movie Maker.*

* * * * * *

For Sasha (Phoenix),
   whose life began as this work ended.
And for Jason and Jodi,
   who were there all the while.

Chronology

1935 Peter Watkins born in Norbiton, Surrey, on October 29.
1947 Attends the College of Christ, a Welsh public school.
1951 Leaves school to attend the preparatory academy for the Royal Academy of Dramatic Arts.
1953 Attends Royal Academy of Dramatic Arts.
1954 Begins tour of duty in the army.
1956 Demobilized from the army, but decides against pursuing an acting career. Resolves to become a filmmaker and makes *The Web* in 8mm.
1958 Makes *The Field of Red*, his first 16mm film.
1959 Directs *The Diary of an Unknown Soldier*. Joins World-wide Pictures, a production company specializing in sponsored documentaries.
1961 Directs *The Forgotten Faces*, his most successful amateur film.
1963 Joins the BBC as an assistant producer.
1964 Directs *Culloden*, his first professional film.
1965 Directs *The War Game*. Resigns from the BBC, in part because of the BBC's refusal to telecast the film.
1966 The BBC finally allows *The War Game* to be seen in cinemas. Watkins begins shooting *Privilege* in August.
1967 *The War Game* wins the Academy Award for best documentary. *Privilege* released in April. Works on script for *Proper in the Circumstances* (unrealized project).
1968 Leaves England and moves to Sweden. Directs *The Gladiators*. First sees the paintings of Edvard Munch.
1969 Moves to the United States and writes *State of the Union*, a script about the American Civil War.
1970 Directs *Punishment Park*.

1971 Moves to Oslo and begins work on a film dealing with the life of Edvard Munch.

1972-
1973 Continues work on *Edvard Munch*.

1974 Moves to Copenhagen. Directs *The 70s People*. November 12-13, first telecast of *Edvard Munch*.

1975 Directs a videoplay, *The Trap*, for Swedish television.

1976 Directs *Evening Land* in Denmark. September, *Edvard Munch* opens in New York City.

1977 Begins research on proposed film biographies of the Russian composer Alexander Scriabin and the Italian poet Filippo Tommaso Marinetti.

1978 Undertakes media research project in Australia and is instrumental in establishing The Peoples' Commission, "a working committee of concerned citizens" living in the Sydney area.

1979 Begins work on a feature film about August Strindberg. The project will be funded by the Swedish Film Institute.

1

Watkins' Early Years: The Amateur Films

PERHAPS because Peter Watkins' films involve disturbing social and political dimensions, the dominant personal quality of his work has been largely ignored beyond the obvious recognition of a particular interview style and a level of intensity which is usually dismissed as "hysterical." The fact remains, however, that Watkins is one of the most personal filmmakers working today.

Like George Orwell, Watkins is concerned about a repressive world order, the suppression of individual freedoms, and the dangerous spread of a soothing conformity, and, for both men, these preoccupations grew not only from the astute observation and analysis of our society but from painful personal experiences as well. Orwell's oppressive school experiences at St. Cyprian's Preparatory School and his tour of duty with the Indian Imperial Police in Burma contributed much to shape his social and political vision. Indeed, a careful reading of "Such, Such Were the Joys" shows how many of the methods of terror and subjection found in the world of 1984 simply extend the techniques employed by Sim and Bingo during his school days. Watkins' school situation was little different from Orwell's, but his childhood terrors were further heightened by the wartime experience of living close to London during the blitz.

Watkins was born on October 29, 1935, in Norbiton, Surrey. His mother did part-time secretarial work, and his father was employed by the Bank of England until the outbreak of the war. At that time, Peter was evacuated along with his mother and younger brother Paul, while his father spent the entire war at sea as a naval coder on a mine sweeper. During the last years of the war, Mrs. Watkins and her sons returned to Surrey

17

The hanging sequence from the never-completed Dust Fever.

and to a life dominated by the constant threat of German bombings. According to Watkins, certain experiences from this period of his life played a significant role in his later psychological development.

I remember many nights spent under the Morrison table which took the place of the traditional dining room table. It had a steel top, reinforced steel and wire mesh all the way around the sides to prevent flying glass entering. And there many Southern English families spent their nights crouched under the table. I remember many nights like this. I remember the bombers droning overhead. I remember the V-I "doodlebug" bomber especially, futting overhead, sounding like a lawn mower and then cutting its engines. At that point, one knew it was falling to earth. I remember those silences often. I remember the rising and falling notes of the sirens. I remember seeing black clouds from antiaircraft shells above the house. Our windows were caved in with concussion at one time. We picked up the fin from a bomb in the garden. All this I suppose was an average experience for a suburban Londoner living on the outskirts during the bombardment, but I still remember it.[1]

After attending a typical elementary school, Watkins was sent, at the age of twelve, to a Welsh public school called the College of Christ, in the county of Brecon. Like so many English boys before him, he was quickly initiated into the traditional methods of schooling for gentlemen: floggings by teachers, a sparse diet, bullying by older boys, and an undue emphasis on the importance of cricket and rugby football in the development of one's competitive spirit. The only "bright spot" during Watkins' four and a half years in Wales was his participation in the school's amateur acting society, where he was often given the leading role in plays performed for the public.

As a result of his interest in theatre, Watkins left the College of Christ at age sixteen to attend the preparatory academy for the Royal Academy of Dramatic Arts. He then spent one full term at RADA itself, but in March, 1954, his studies were interrupted by a compulsory tour of duty in the army. He was drafted into the East Surrey Regiment and sent to Canterbury, where he was again bullied severely because he was considered officer material and, therefore, capable of taking this kind of treatment. After being injured on an obstacle assault course at an officer selection training school, he was returned to Canterbury, where he was placed on a draft of the Queen's Regiment which was scheduled to depart for Kenya to fight the Mau Maus. Fortunately, after scoring highest in a course for clerk's training, Watkins applied for and obtained a position as clerk in the Brigade Quarters and served the remainder of his tour of duty in Canterbury.

The alienation which Watkins experienced at public school and in the army was alleviated in both cases through participation in dramatic groups. While at Canterbury, he joined the Amateur Dramatic Society and subsequently became a member of Playcraft, a small group which performed plays in the dining room of the home of June and Alan Grey. Aside from acting in a number of Playcraft productions, Watkins also directed *Journey's End*, R. C. Sherriff's play about trench warfare during World War I. It is significant that Watkins chose this particular play to direct, since its themes of the stupidity of war and the horrible psychological and physical effects on those involved became especially important concerns in his amateur and early professional films.

Watkins left the army in 1956, but decided against pursuing an acting career. Soon after making this decision, he saw an amateur film which detailed a Socialist demonstration in the town of Herne Bay, in Kent. Almost immediately, he purchased an 8 mm camera and resolved to become a filmmaker. Although he now lived with his parents in Surrey, Watkins still kept in close contact with the Playcraft group, which had been taken over by Stan and Phil Mercer, and one of his earliest filming efforts was to shoot footage of their production of *The Glass Menagerie*. A short time later, he solicited the assistance of Playcraft in making an ambitious 8 mm film entitled *The Web*.

This short film, which was awarded a Gold Star in the Ten Best Amateur Films competition of 1956, depicts the plight of a Nazi soldier attempting to escape from the forces of the French underground. The emphasis is on this man's alienation. After the death of his friend, he wanders over the French countryside (actually fields near Canterbury) until he confronts a young woman who, instead of betraying his presence, attempts to get him water. This act of human kindness contrasts sharply with the actions of the maquis who, rather than capturing the German, make him walk away from them so that they can playfully shoot him in the back. At the very end of the film, the young woman discovers the body of the soldier who is still clutching the handkerchief she had given him.

A key Watkins theme, the need for people to care about other human beings on an individual level, stands behind *The Web*, and, in a way, the encounter in this film prefigures the relationship between B4 and the Chinese girl in *The Gladiators*. Much in *The Web*, however, is clichéd and heavy-handed, including a number of symbolic set scenes, such as the scratching and rubbing out of a cross in the sand. Also the film reveals a beginner's failure to understand rhythm and pacing. There are too many far shots of the German soldier running across fields, and often these shots continue long after the audience has absorbed all the visual information contained in the shot.

Watkins quickly learned the power of editing when he joined George Street and Company, a London advertising agency, where he worked as an assistant producer responsible for making 30- and 60-second spots for commercial television. "We became in a sense like directors, and we were responsible for a great deal. I and my colleagues were continually running to recording studios, to laboratories. It was a fantastic experience. I *hated* advertising, but the experience was fantastic. We even had to recut ourselves several longer films. Half-hour documentaries on how port wine is produced. . . . These kinds of things."

With a steady job and a growing commitment to amateur filmmaking, Watkins purchased a used Ensign Kinecam and switched to a 16 mm format. His first production in 16 mm was *The Field of Red* (1958), an unsuccessful film about the American Civil War. Unfortunately, the only print of this film has not survived. The failure of *The Field of Red*, however, failed to dampen Watkins' enthusiasm, and he quickly began work on a new project. *The Diary of an Unknown Soldier* (1959) is a remarkable amateur film by any standard, but from the perspective of hindsight, its importance to Watkins' development as a filmmaker cannot be overestimated.

Unlike most American directors who were rarely involved in the amateur film scene, British directors often used their amateur films as stepping stones to professional careers. John Schlesinger, Ken Russell, and Peter Watkins were all hired by the BBC on the basis of their amateur films, and many of these films reveal much about their later styles as feature filmmakers. The use of crowds, for instance, in John Schlesinger's first amateur film, *Black Legend* (1948), is markedly similar to the construction of crowd scenes in *Far From the Madding Crowd* (1967); and Ken Russell's camera choreography and experiments with music to define mood and reinforce theme appear as early as *Amelia and the Angel* (1957). In *The Diary of an Unknown Soldier*, however, Watkins initiated a style of filmmaking which he has consistently developed and experimented with in all of his professional films.

The Diary of an Unknown Soldier deals with some of the same themes found in *Journey's End*, but whereas Sherriff allowed the conventions of the stage to limit his action to a claustrophobic dugout in the British trenches before St. Quentin, Watkins refused to be constrained by comparable cinematic conventions. Even at this stage of his career, he was quick to understand the nature of his medium; in this film, he freed the camera from the limitations of a fixed vantage point and forced it to take part in the action so that he could create strikingly realistic, almost newsreellike, effects and directly in-

Allied soldiers wait for orders to attack the German lines in *The Diary of an Unknown Soldier.*

volve the viewing audience in the events it was witnessing. *The Diary of an Unknown Soldier*, however, is not limited strictly to techniques of realism. It contains a curious, almost uneasy, mixture of expressionist and documentary styles, and one suspects that the financial and physical limitations that Watkins faced because of equipment and location problems played a major part in the evolution of this syncretistic approach. Synchronous sound was not possible for financial reasons; little of the surrounding countryside near Canterbury resembled the trenches of World War I, and a cast of fifteen to twenty had to give the illusion of being five times that number.

A carefully written script for the film existed before any footage was shot; and, after the film was edited, Watkins added an optical soundtrack of realistic effects and a commentary—presumably from the diary of the nameless protagonist who is about to face the front for the first time. The opening line of the film, "last day of my life," establishes the narrator's bizarre perspective and even suggests the film's expressionist mood. The remainder of the commentary complements and clarifies the film's visuals, and the rapid pace at which Watkins himself speaks these lines creates a sense of relentless urgency that reflects the protagonist's constant condition of tension. Occasionally, the pace is a bit too frantic. As a result, some images (trees metamorphosing into bayonets) seem to be a clichéd imitation of Sergei Eisenstein's techniques. Also, certain overly emotional sections from the commentary ("The most terrible thing about war is not just the fact that we have to kill men so much like ourselves, but that we have to hate them and keep on hating them. . . . It seems so bloody pointless. We go forward to those guns. God only knows what will happen to us. God only knows") reduce rather than increase the impact of the film's message. In all of his future films, with the exception of *Evening Land* (1977), Watkins would employ some form of narration, but never again in this obvious, didactic manner.

The strength of *The Diary of an Unknown Soldier* rests with its striking visual impact. Much of the film, photographed by Watkins himself, consists of close-ups and extreme close-ups of the protagonist or what the viewer sees from his perspective. These shots are noteworthy because of Watkins' unique framing. He frequently frames the top of the shot below the hair line rather than cropping at the top of the head in what is often called a "Warner Brothers close-up." Indeed, Watkins intentionally creates disturbing shots in this film by ignoring a standard rule which indicates that a proper balance for large close-ups is achieved by framing the subject's eyes just above the imaginary horizontal center. Throughout his early career, Watkins experimented with this type of framing, and by the time he made *Punishment Park* (1970), he had come to definite conclusions about the framing of close-up shots. "Normally the weight of most camera and most television shots is down-loaded. You always see air over the heads [in Hollywood films]. . . . I close the air off over the head to stop the strength of the scene going out. You can see more of the body. The whole thing is very much solid, and you are forced to look at the person—into their eyes."[2]

Most of the other shots of the soldiers in the film are close-middle shots, and the frequency of this kind of shot was probably dictated in part by the limited number of cast members and by problems with location. The sequence depicting soldiers leaping into the mud of "no man's land" as they advance toward the German lines, for instance, was filmed in a cast member's backyard, after an eight-foot-square plot had been dug up and hosed down with water. Watkins, however, had more in mind than simply making do with what was available. By moving the camera in an adventurous manner, he made it a "participant" in the battle sequences. As Tony Rose, Britain's foremost amateur film authority, wisely observed, ". . . he went in close with his camera, filled the frame with writhing bodies and hurtling feet, allowed the lens to be jostled and jumped over and practically trodden into the mud. The result was magnificent and it looked like war as the soldier sees it."[3] This aspect of the film impressed others as well, and Watkins won an "Oscar" in the Ten Best Amateur Films Competition of 1959.

Also in 1959, Watkins left the firm of George Street and Company and joined World-wide Pictures, a film production company which specialized in making sponsored documentaries. Here he worked closely with Kevin Brownlow, who went on to make *It Happened Here* (in which Watkins plays a German soldier), and with John Trumper, an editor who

worked with John Grierson's Group Three Productions and
who later served as editor for Watkins' own first cinema feature, *Privilege*. After about a year at World-wide as an assistant
editor working on both 16 and 35 mm sound-sync productions,
Watkins became an editor. Then in 1961, he served as a director for two sponsored films: one made in Libya for the Ford
Motor Company and one on British air traffic control for the
Civil Aviation Board. According to Watkins, "they were half-
hour films which shall remain nameless. One was with
dialogue (the air traffic control film), and one was without.
They were very stylized, and I probably would be very
ashamed of them now. They were very rudimentary, but . . .
while I am making those, I am making *The Forgotten Faces* at
the same time—which is an infinitely more important film and
more important to me."

Part of the reason for the importance of this film stems from
the fact that it was a reaction against the stylization and "regu-
lation professional manner" of the type of films that Watkins
was making for World-wide. *The Forgotten Faces* (1961), a
film reconstruction of the Hungarian revolution of 1956, won
Watkins another amateur Oscar, and to this day, the film is
praised in England as "one of the most memorable amateur
films ever made."

The Forgotten Faces advanced the methods of realistic reconstruction that he initiated in the *The Diary of an Unknown
Soldier*. Surely, Kevin Brownlow must have supplied some
encouragement in this direction, since, like Watkins, he also
worked at World-wide in part to fund his own film project
about what would have happened in England had the Nazis
taken over. Watkins also found some inspiration in Truffaut's
Les Quatre Cents Coups and in the work of the Italian neo-re-
alist directors who, if they did not attempt to capture a newsreel effect, at least frequently used nonprofessionals in location sequences filmed with available lighting. The films of
Rossellini, de Sica, Olmi, and early Visconti, however, had little direct influence on Watkins' dismissal of traditional
cinematic artifice in his attempts to realistically recreate
events.

Most of my feelings about this kind of what I would call documentary or reconstruction of reality came from studying photographs. I
think that's where my feelings about grain and people looking into

the camera came from . . . especially those very strong photographs taken in the streets of Budapest and published in *Paris Match* and *Life*. That was my first in-depth encounter with an actual situation. I studies [*sic*] hundreds of photographs to try to recapture the feel in film.[4]

The "feel" of these photographs permeates *The Forgotten Faces* as the close-ups of students, workers, children, and grandmothers stare out from the frame and incorporate us, the audience, into their world. The effectiveness of this technique depends, to some extent, on the editing and on the convincing nature of the street sequences, most of which are filmed in long and far shots. During these sequences, the camera is jostled, jerked, and occasionally thrown out of focus as it moves through the action and records an ambush by police snipers, the wrecking of a vehicle disguised as a Red Cross truck, the execution of three members of the Soviet-controlled secret police, the flight of an escaping freedom fighter, and the stringing up of a man by his feet after the storming of party headquarters. Similar techniques are used in capturing intimate expressions of grief and quiet moments when the members of the revolutionary forces (students, workers, and soldiers) argue their diverse political views. In fact, the only false note in the entire film occurs during a sequence in which Watkins uses a soundtrack of stirring Hungarian music as the background to a young girl reading one of her articles which has been published in a revolutionary newspaper. The details of the scene and the composition of the shots evoke Sergei Eisentein's *October*, and while the allusion is not gratuitous, it detracts from the film's overall effect.

Aside from this sequence, Watkins communicates the sensation that the camera is recording events as they actually happen because, as Tony Rose notes, he successfully breaks two deep-rooted cinematic conventions – the pretenses that actors do not see the camera and that an "invisible observer always knows what is going to happen next so that it [the camera] is always pointing in the right direction, correctly focused and framing the picture nicely."[5] In *The Forgotten Faces*, the camera is fooled or surprised and must be quickly brought into focus. Also, its presence is almost always noticed by the people being filmed. Watkins has these faces of the inhabitants of Budapest stare out at us not so much to arouse our

Faces of Hungarian revolutionaries

from *The Forgotten Faces*.

sympathy as to reinforce one of his dominant themes which is verbally articulated by the narrator near the end of the film.

There has to be a right and wrong in any human conflict. This most tragic of revolutions can be no exception. But in any conflict between two major creeds, one of which you believe in, there has to be a final taking of sides. And if those who happened to believe, as these Hungarian freedom fighters believed, had taken a strong moral stand on their behalf at a time when it most mattered, then it is more than likely that more than 20,000 of these people need not have given their lives or their liberty for this belief.

The Forgotten Faces is not a one-sided, simplistic political tract. Watkins is clearly sympathetic to the revolutionaries, but still his camera and narrator do not refrain from revealing some of the atrocities carried out by mobs seeking revenge on members of the A. V. H. (secret police). The commentary even goes so far as to raise serious questions about the possible behavior of the revolutionaries had they won. "If the freedom fighters had actually won the revolution, would any of them have donned similar uniforms to hold these men [members of the A.V.H.] in check?" In the final analysis, Watkins' film convincingly depicts a situation in which numerous people died as the result of the failure of others to take "a strong stand." As such, the film is not simply about an historic event; it is an appeal to us, the audience, to take positions, to give expression to our feelings and beliefs when it is necessary for us to do so. With this film, Watkins began his commitment to rouse us from the false security of our blissful apathy, and while his career has been plagued with frustration and personal hardships, he has never lost sight of this intention nor abandoned his belief in the dignity of the individual who defies the forces of a repressive society.

Watkins may not have formulated all of his reasons for wanting to be a filmmaker at the time he was making *The Forgotten Faces*, but he knew that he wanted to experiment further with the techniques of realistic reconstruction. The directing of large-scale amateur productions also made him realize that filmmaking under certain circumstances can be a gratifying communal experience and that amateurs when given a special framework can achieve levels of intensity and enthusiasm missing from more conventional ways of making films.

The enthusiasm and intensity which abounded during the nine days of shooting *The Forgotten Faces* resulted, in part, from the participation of most of the members of Playcraft, which formed the core of the cast. The chief location for the film was a dead-end street in Canterbury which contained the city's abandoned gas works, and to make the area resemble a Budapest street in late October, 1956, small trees were wired to the pavement and piles of rubble were carted in. The shooting was nonstop during daylight hours, and since the script was never completed, Watkins improvised as necessity or good fortune dictated. At one point, for instance, a tourist passed by on his way to a nearby chapel. In a matter of minutes, he was in a soldier's uniform and thrust against a wall about to be shot. In the final film, this sequence is especially effective because of the tourist's uncanny resemblance to one of the A.V.H. men depicted in John Sadovy's famous photograph of the actual incident. There were no speaking roles for any of the participants, with the exception of the narrator's commentary which was added after the film was edited, so Watkins simply worked with his cast in terms of movement and facial expressions. Finally, after exposing over sixty minutes of film, Watkins spent months editing down his material to its final form of seventeen minutes.[6]

After the success of *The Forgotten Faces*, Watkins attempted to make another amateur production—a film entitled *Dust Fever*, conceived as a reaction against conventional Hollywood Westerns. While Watkins succeeded in filming characters who looked real enough, the story ("A bawdy, feverish, lusty, quick-tempered and tragic slice of America's west-seaboard history")[7] never transcended some of the clichés of the genre. The film was shot in a stone quarry near Canterbury, and, while the budget was considerably higher than his other amateur films, Watkins never achieved more than a rough cut of the film. What he did achieve, however, was a communal atmosphere which existed beyond the level of artistic cooperation established during the filming session. The warmth and fellowship associated with all the amateur productions, but in particular *Dust Fever*, are still fondly remembered by former members of Playcraft who live in Canterbury.

Not only was this period "the happiest" in his entire career as a filmmaker, but, for Watkins, the amateur years were essential. Without them, his work in film most certainly would have taken an entirely different direction. "I think not only did my work artistically stem from my experiences as an amateur, but I think that my ability to fight, to stick it out, and to develop and pursue my own kind of personal vision . . . has its roots in that experience."[8]

2

The BBC Years:
Culloden and *The War Game*

ON THE BASIS OF *The Forgotten Faces*, Huw Wheldon, head of Documentary Programming, hired Peter Watkins as an assistant producer for the BBC in 1963. During the year that Watkins held this position, he worked on a number of productions, the most notable of which was Stephen Hearst's *The Life and Times of Marshal Tito*.

Culloden

The early 1960s were an especially adventuresome and artistically exciting period at the BBC, and although Watkins' first attempt to make a film about the effects of a nuclear attack on Britain was shelved, his proposal to make *Culloden* was encouraged. This film, which graphically depicts the last battle fought on British soil and the resulting destruction of the Scottish Highland clans after the 1745-1746 Jacobite uprising, had been originally conceived as an amateur production. The BBC, however, in no way forced him to revise his methods of filmmaking. "Huw Wheldon said, 'Well just do it.' I don't think he had time or particularly wanted to read the script; he just let me do it. It was completely subjective, of course, as those were the golden days of documentaries; I am not sure that the freedom I had exists any more. But it was marvelous at that time. Unfortunately, Huw Wheldon went up to his high position, and the situation has changed."[1]

Making *Culloden* for the BBC allowed Watkins to have John Prebble serve as the film's historical advisor and to draw freely from Prebble's excellent history of the battle. As an adaptation of Prebble's book, Watkins' film succeeds admirably in capturing the theme and much of the tone of the original

Culloden: British troops examine one of the many Scots slaughtered on the road to Inverness.

work. The film even loosely follows the structure of Prebble's account. For instance, the opening and conclusion of the book are closely paralleled in the film. Finally, Watkins used actual lines of dialogue from the text, while condensing and finding visual equivalents for Prebble's pages of background information and verbal description.

Watkins claims that, even with BBC sponsorship, *Culloden* was still made in exactly the manner it would have been done had the film been an amateur effort. This means that he used ordinary people for all roles, an unblimped 16 mm Arriflex camera (usually hand held), and an interview method which forced the "actors" to directly confront the camera and, by extension, the audience. At first some of the BBC technicians who worked on the film were skeptical of Watkins' methods. Dick Bush, one of the BBC's best cameramen, was selected to shoot *Culloden*, and he had grave misgivings about the project. Once the actual shooting began, however, Bush quickly changed his opinion. "I viewed the forthcoming production of *Culloden* with a bit of apprehension. I wasn't quite sure that Peter's approach was the right one, but I thought, 'Well, we will see how things go.' We went up to Scotland to shoot the production, and I hadn't been working with him for more than an hour, when I realized that I was the one who had the limitations and that Peter was quite brilliant in his conception of the film."[2]

The brilliance of Watkins' conceptions and the fact that this film would alter traditional conceptions of filmic reconstructions were recognized by many critics immediately after the film was telecast on BBC 1 on December 15, 1964. Adrian Mitchell in *The Sun* praised the film as "one of the bravest documentaries"; Mary Crozier in *The Guardian* acknowledged the film to be "an unforgettable experiment . . . that was new and adventurous in technique," and the reviewer in *The Observer* simply called the film a "breakthrough." Although it was recognized by the Society of Film and Television Arts with an award and Watkins was given the British Screen Writers' Award of Merit, *Culloden* was attacked in a few quarters as a "sadistic and revolting programme" which greatly disturbed the viewing public.[3] Also, soon after its initial screening, Equity, the actor's union, protested the use of non-professional actors in the film.

The reasons for the overwhelmingly favorable critical response to *Culloden* are not difficult to pinpoint. Although the BBC allowed new directors all kinds of freedom during the early sixties, many of the documentaries of the period remained staid and stodgy because the BBC was still uneasy about dramatized documentaries which used actors to impersonate people who had actually lived. *Culloden*, needless to say, pushed far beyond the conventional BBC fare and also introduced a kind of graphic realism which created a shattering impact on many viewers. Beyond that, the film was a technically superior work with excellent production values, especially when one considers a low television budget, the actual number of people in the cast, and the limited use of props—including just one cannon for the entire filming. Finally, *Culloden* was a film which could be viewed on a number of different levels, and, as such, according to Watkins, it emerges as his "safest" film.

This last observation can be borne out by the fact that it has been used as a study film for a course in military history on a United States Army base in Kansas, and even the discussion of the film on the PBS network after its 1973 screening on the Humanities Film Series emphasized the accuracy of the reconstruction rather than the far-reaching implications of the film. For too many viewers the film is merely an expert delineation of tragic events from the distant past; and although the methods employed in the film almost guarantee some kind of emotional involvement, some viewers fail to make the implicit connections with the present. Watkins now thinks that such a response to the film is all too common.

Culloden . . . can be responded to on the level of armchair, white liberal discomfort at a historical event. It was not intended to be taken on this level, but I know that a lot of people accept it this way; that, I think, is the reason for its popularity. People can say, *Culloden*, oh yes, that's a fantastic film, look what they did in those times, isn't war bad! But although the film does affect us all—and I think all of us can see ourselves in the faces of those people at that time—I think there is a mental loophole so that you can also say that you don't. It just sits at that edge of the definition where a white, middle-class liberal—and in fact a broader area even than that—can sort of indulge in the cathartic exercise of looking at something, getting a kick out of it, washing his guilt off, and then getting on with the dishes afterwards.[4]

Still, although Watkins now sees *Culloden* as a film which fell below his expectations, the film's impact forces most viewers to become involved, even if only momentarily, in the horror of the events they are watching.

One of the more obvious devices that Watkins uses to instigate audience involvement is the heightened sense of realism achieved through the newsreel quality of the film, but it is not enough to describe *Culloden* as a newsreel imitation using a "You Are There" approach. The film, on every level, is far too complex for such a facile generalization. First of all, its major technique is not simply a reworking of the old Walter Cronkite television show in which reporters select their subjects and some of their questions from the pseudo-omniscient perspective of the present. If that were the case, Watkins' film, like the Cronkite series, would reflect the artificiality of this kind of canned "instant" history. In *Culloden*, even though the narrator speaks at times from the perspective of history, he occupies a multifaceted role, and the off-screen interviewer (another voice altogether) is always firmly placed in the past. Secondly, unlike the Cronkite series, Watkins uses interview situations in a number of unique ways to insure responses from his audience. His special technique of using close-ups so that the characters on the screen do not ignore the camera was taken over from *The Forgotten Faces*, and thus when the rain-soaked, ill-fed Highlanders gaze into the lens, they seem to be directly confronting us—the audience. Also, the techniques of jolting the hand-held camera during bombardment sequences and the frequent readjustment of focus of long focal lenses to break down the necessary conventions of theatrical films were carried over from the amateur films.

Watkins' methods in *Culloden*, then, extended on a larger scale those techniques employed in his best amateur films. He simply attempted to build up "a tapestry of things that create the feeling of a spontaneous recording on film of something that is happening. It's a technique learned from newsreels and it's not at all easy to do. It has a very high failure ratio."[5] As such, all his films, even those at this stage of his career, have high shooting ratios, and often the different takes concern various camera movements rather than just attempts to capture the best response from a nonprofessional actor.

It must be noted, however, that beyond a superficial comparison, Watkins' methods have little in common with the so-called spontaneous, unstructured filmmaking associated with *cinéma-vérité*. Watkins tries to create a heightened sense of reality through the use of hand-held cameras, flat, untheatrical lighting, nonprofessional actors, direct sound recording, and seemingly impromptu interviews, but unlike the practitioners of direct cinema, who use many of these same methods to break down barriers between the subject and the camera and to get at "the whole truth," Watkins' concerns also extend to breaking down barriers between the film and the audience. Also, his attitudes toward "truth" and "history" are so complex that he would never suggest that his films reflect the "whole truth." This does not mean, however, that they should be considered fabrications, which unfortunately is a charge brought against all of his work, including *Culloden*. Watkins, unlike *cinéma-vérité* filmmakers, does not try to make his nonprofessional actors ignore the existence of the camera, and he does not rely on minimum or simple editing procedures to establish chronological time. His involved methods of editing have grown with each film, and in his most recent work, he has totally dismissed chronological time as a viable organizing principle. Rather, the extensive use of counterpointing and complex sound transitions in Watkins' editing procedures have come to reflect the very tensions which are so much an integral part of the rhythms of his films. Finally, unlike those involved in direct cinema, Watkins depends on and experiments with a narrator who is of major importance in establishing audience perspectives.

As such, Watkins' films are syncretistic and unique unto him; they make use of various techniques from styles as divergent as realism and expressionism—usually in an attempt to generate a meaningful audience response. In *Culloden*, however, Watkins also fell back on standard, conventional effects often used by filmmakers who wish to jolt an audience. Thus, he makes occasional use of a particularly graphic shot or consciously sets up a shock cut to startle the audience. For instance, there is the shot of a Highlander hacking away with his sword at a British soldier who suddenly whirls close to the camera to reveal his slashed eyes. There is also the freeze frame medium-shot of the mortally wounded Walter Stapleton, commander of the Irish Pickets. More than just serving as a shock shot, however, this freeze frame condenses time in that Stapleton's death symbolically represents the cutting down of the entire Irish brigade.

As previously discussed, the frequent use of close-up shots—especially of the Highlanders—forces the members of the audience to respond to the people on the screen, and the shots of the violence and the aftermath are carefully calculated to gain sympathy, so much so that the director even occasionally breaks away from the newsreel effect to place the viewer in the perspective of various characters. Witness the Scottish Highlanders who lie wounded on the battlefield long after their defeat, especially the one whose point of view the audience shares as he is carried off by British soldiers, dropped on the ground, and summarily executed.

The lack of panoramic shots, so often encountered in films which depict battle scenes, is especially notable in *Culloden*. Such shots would not have concealed the fact that Watkins usually employed no more than fifty people to suggest several thousand. Also, given his purposes for this film, isolated scenes of horror and violence (often filmed in tight close-middle or carefully framed long shots) are far more effective in creating tension and intensity than massive large-scale battle sequences with panoramic shots.

Even more impressive, however, is the director's superb use of the narrator (Watkins himself) who fulfills multiple functions as he skillfully shifts from one role to another often without the slightest detection. The interviews with participants of the battle are conducted by another off-screen voice, and the authenticity of on-the-spot historical observation is provided by an actor portraying Andrew Henderson, the Whig historian. For some critics, the use of Henderson to comment on the logistics of the battle stands as the one obvious, artificial device in the film, but minor as his role is, he remains an observer with a personality and perhaps, as such, is a precursor of sorts to the "involved" television journalist in *Punishment Park*. In any event, in *Culloden* it is the narrator who commands our attention and deserves a more detailed investigation. With Henderson and another off-screen voice to provide an on-the-spot ambience, the narrator is free to serve as storyteller, factual annotator, ironic commentator, sympathetic partisan, and, on at least one occasion, omniscient observer.

The point of view in the film constantly shifts in slight, subtle ways even while emphasizing "the facts" as presented by a narrator who is from our own age. The confidence of the audience in the narrator is generally assured because of his special vantage point, but Watkins has never argued that his films are objective, and thus he presents many of his own personal attitudes through the narrator.

First of all, the narrator is a storyteller whose thematic concerns are best revealed in the written text introducing the film:

An account of the most mishandled and brutal battle ever fought in Britain.

An account of its tragic aftermath.

An account of the men responsible for it.

An account of the men, women and children who suffered because of it.

These events actually happened, and to insure that the audience always remains conscious that it is not just listening to a story, the narrator also provides a frequent annotation of facts. In a detached manner, he lists the names and numbers of men

Members of the Highland clans.

found in various regiments and clans, along with precise times, distances, kinds of weapons, and battle instructions. This manner of presentation, however, when combined with images selected by the filmmaker, creates an effect which is anything but detached. For instance, the narrator (much in the style of an educational demonstration film) tells of cast-iron balls of three pounds weight being loaded into a cannon. "This is round shot. This is what it does." The image on the screen of young men being blown apart graphically illustrates its use. Thus, even when the narrator seems to be removed from any kind of partisan response, the linking of his voice to certain images pushes him toward what he openly becomes by the end of the film—the moral spokesman through which the audience comes to judge the activities depicted. In the first half of the film, much of the commentary is devoted to "detached" factual observations, but obvious subjective responses are also present. Witness the narrator's description of Joshua Ward, who, as a lieutenant in the British army, belongs to "a fraternity where the least pretension to learning, propriety, or common morals would endanger the owner to be cashiered."

The narrator at times also assumes a posture of omniscience when he delineates the thought processes of certain historical characters. While a close-up of Prince Charles Edward Stuart appears on the screen, the narrator informs the audience that Charles claims "that only those who are afraid can doubt his coming victory. He puts from his mind the discontent of the MacDonalds, the fatigue and hunger of his men, the total outnumbering of his army, the thinning of ranks by desertion, the ill choice of battle field—convinced as he is of the invincibility of his men."

In the second half of the film, the narrator's use of such phrases as "pacification" to describe the policies of the duke of Cumberland, William Augustus, and the specific reference to "police action" by Lord Sackville demand comparisons between the past and the present. Indeed, the genocide practiced by the British on the Highland clans should evoke the atrocities of the Vietnamese war. Finally, in the closing moments of the film, the narrator sheds all vestiges of detachment and delivers his most eloquent statement—this time staunchly in the role of moral spokesman:

The year of the Prince had ended, but for the English government it was just beginning. Systematically and with due parliamentary legislation, they proceeded to eliminate all the things that made this man unique and gave him the strength they so feared. They penalized the wearing of his Highland dress, penalized the weaving of his Highland tartan, penalized the worshipping at his Church, penalized the carrying of his weapons, penalized the playing of his music. They removed the authority of his chief, and in one blow smashed forever the system of his clan. They then encouraged his chief to lose interest in him, to evict him, and to replace him by the more profitable sheep. Thus they reduced him to a nameless, unwanted oddity, and finally forced him in his hundreds of thousands to leave the land of his birth for the canning industries of the North, for the disease-ridden slums of the South, for the lumber camps of Canada and the stockyards of Australia. And wherever he went, he took with him his music, his poetry, his language, and his children.

Thus within a century from Culloden, the British and the Scottish Lowlanders had made secure forever their religion, their commerce, their culture, their ruling dynasty and, in so doing, destroyed a race of people. They have created a desert and called it peace.

If the narrator is one of the centers of consciousness in Watkins' films, then the other, as critic Bruce Kawin indicates,[6] is the cameraman who seems to be on-the-spot recording the events as they occur. The success of this method involves more than giving us the perspective of the cameraman as he is jolted, jostled, evaded, and confronted; more than treating the face as a human landscape; and more than structuring interviews to simulate on-the-street encounters. For this method to work, the director must have an intuitive sense of selecting nonprofessionals whose actions will appear natural and whose facial expressions will convey various emotional extremes. Watkins, like Sergei Eisenstein, who sought out certain facial types when casting his silent films, clearly recognized the importance of his choices.

The fact that I get somebody who looks right is more important to me than getting somebody who might be qualified to play the part mentally because I can work on the mental performance afterwards and for the television screen you need immediate impact; you have to make your point hard and fast on that little box. Of course, when it comes to the clansmen who are really the backbone of this film, you have no historical likenesses to follow, so then you can go after marvelous faces and people who have got something extra. We had people coming on the moor where we were filming and we would take them away, stain their bodies with iodine, put wigs and bonnets on them and suddenly they took on a roughness.... they became their ancestors.[7]

More is needed for a successful film, however, than merely the right facial types. A supportive relationship must exist between the director and his actors. "If you go up to a child of twelve or a woman of eighty and give them something to do which is within the bounds of their own characters and their own experiences, then you can reduce them to tears, you can get a performance of pathos, you can get anything you like from them as long as you handle them carefully."[8]

Watkins' phrasing here deserves some comment. Even at this early stage of his development as a filmmaker, his concern is with using nonprofessionals who will be able to perform in a manner that is within the limits of their own characters and experiences. This working from experiences within the actors themselves becomes even more important in his later films where characterization becomes much more subtle and complex and where "actors" are asked to improvise dialogue drawn from their own feelings.

In the making of *Culloden*, however, Watkins notes that there was little time "to explain the whole situation" because most of the people had other jobs to do and were only available for severely limited periods of time.

In that short time, you have to whip something exciting and interesting out of him, so you tend to forget the niceties and ... smash him into shape in a few minutes which is a ruthless system, but it does work. And you have to maintain a sense of proportion. If you want a shot of a man grovelling in fear, you don't necessarily have to tell him the whole history of his regiment. You just get him into a state of fear in five minutes by telling him the situation within that five minutes and then proceed to get it out of him.[9]

This method clearly worked for *Culloden* and *The War Game* where many of the characters are, to a great extent, simply representatives of people in a specific set of circumstances. That is to say, they are minimally developed characters with limited speaking roles whose own personality backgrounds are frequently unnecessary given the specific contexts in which we encounter them in the film. With *Privilege* the speaking roles are substantially increased, and beginning with *Edvard Munch*, most of the people in Watkins' films exist as unique individuals as well as representatives of people in various circumstances. As such, Watkins has spent much more time with them in discussing, not simply his reasons for making the film, but their own feelings about the issues the film raises and the situations in which they find themselves as the characters in the film.

Even as early as *Culloden*, however, Watkins attempted to make the cast members understand the film's "connection with them as human beings" and to provide a meaningful, common experience for those in the film. The selection of participants in his early films usually took place at mass meetings of interested townspeople. During these meetings, Watkins explained the nature of the film and his purpose in making it, and then he met briefly with each person individually: "I have an idea of the sort of people I am trying to cast but it has to be immensely flexible. If I see a guy who I think might be a good policeman, I make a note of that; I talk to each person for about ten minutes or a quarter of an hour; it depends on the time pressures."[10]

It must be emphasized that unlike some other directors who have used amateur actors, Watkins never tricked anyone into surprised or shocked expressions of horror. He simply sought to involve them as much as possible in the situation depicted in the film. He attempted in *Culloden*, for example, to make those portraying the English soldiers volleying by ranks at the charging Highlanders think about what it would feel like when they realized that they had actually shot someone. Thus, the lowest form of attack on Watkins, rumors which were circulated during *The War Game* controversy perhaps in a misguided attempt to discredit him, involved stories about his "unethical" and "unprofessional" treatment of those who worked on *Culloden*. He was accused of misdirecting the mobile food service so that the actors would look hungry and of using trip wires for realistic falls. Members of the cast were quick to refute these charges, and Watkins himself replied in the following manner: "I have never tripped anyone up in my life or made anyone go hungry. You don't get people to work for you by cheating and hurting them. I know that I can't begin to get any response from an actor—especially an amateur—unless he trusts me completely. If there were any hint of trickery, I'd be finished."[11]

Also essential to Watkins' filmmaking technique in *Culloden* is his use of sound and editing to create tension, ironic impact, and perhaps another perspective beyond those supplied by the narrator and cameraman. Although the editing and use of sound in *Culloden* may not appear especially complex when compared with some of his recent films, they do account for the basic counterpoint rhythm, which provides the film's most obvious organizational structure. Watkins depicts the Scottish forces, then the English, and finally the resulting battle and its aftermath. The sounds of pipes and drums distinguish each army, just as uniforms and types of weapons do on the visual level, but the contrast also extends to the soldiers, officers, and commanders within each army. Thus, the two protagonists, Bonnie Prince Charles and the duke of Cumberland, are seen as kinds of chess players who maneuver their pieces across the battlefield. The clan leaders and the British officers correspond to the more powerful pieces in the game, and the pawns, those lowly figures who carry out the bulk of the fighting, consist of farmers, tradesmen, and cotters. In the British army, the pawns were often pressed into service, and in the Scottish army, they were forced to fight because of a ruthless clan system which demanded human rent as payment for land and privileges. In both cases "the system" eliminated any recognition of the worth of the individual.

Aside from the extended use of crosscutting, Watkins also edited numerous sequences of *Culloden* for ironic effect. Almost every time Bonnie Prince Charlie utters an opinion about the battle, the successive shots contradict his statement. For instance, early in the film, he says that "the people of England will welcome me." Cut to a shot of advancing English soldiers. Later, after his second utterance that "God is on our side," he claims that the English "will never fight me." Cut to a shot of English soldiers fixing bayonets.

While the focus in the first half of the film falls chiefly on the Scots and the bungling of O'Sullivan, the discontent of the MacDonalds, and the utter incompetence of Charles Edward Stuart as a military leader, the focus in the second half falls mainly on the duke of Cumberland and those English officers and soldiers who carry out what is termed "a pacification of

the Highlands." The editing of this section of the film is especially strong in providing bitter ironic commentary on the actions of "an Englishman protecting his liberty and his Protes-
tant religion." When the narrator tells us that "thus has ended
the last battle to be fought in Britain and the last attempt to
overthrow its king. The establishment has been saved; peace
restored; church, crown, trade, and commerce safeguarded,"
the image cuts from a triumphant William Augustus parading
before his troops to a Scottish mother holding the limp body of
her young child. This pattern continues as William lets his regiments of horse loose after the victory "in order that they may
have some sweets with all their fatigue." While the narrator
reads commendations received by James Ray, the first English
soldier to reach Inverness, for "performing many and glorious
exploits," the image shifts from Ray to the results of his
deeds—the bodies of slaughtered, innocent civilians who took
no part in the battle.

After further graphic illustrations of the English raids into
the hills and glens in order, as Cumberland phrases it, "to
wear down this generation until there be peace in the land,"
Watkins shows Bonnie Prince Charlie leaving Scotland for the
safety of France. The film then ends with a long indictment by
the narrator (already quoted in full) and close-ups of faces as
the camera moves slowly down a line of weary Highlanders.

Few filmmakers have begun their professional careers with
such an auspicious work as *Culloden*, and in 1964, no young
filmmaker at the BBC showed more promise than Peter Watkins. Clearly because of the artistic success of his first film, he
was now allowed to begin work on his initially shelved nuclear film.

The War Game

"There are some who would prefer that no risks should be
taken. Many however share the view of the BBC that the effort
should be made.... The BBC should not confine itself to
seeking the comfortable solution of safe programmes that
avoid saying anything provocative by saying virtually nothing
new."

BBC Annual Report of 1965, issued on November 24, 1965
"This is the BBC's own decision. It has been taken after a

good deal of thought and discussion, but not as a result of out-side pressure of any kind. The effect of the film has been judged by the BBC to be too horrifying for the medium of broadcasting."

BBC announcement on *The War Game*, issued on November 26, 1965

*   *   *   *   *

Like *Culloden*, the genesis of *The War Game* can be traced to a project that was conceived as an amateur film. As early as 1961, Watkins planned to make a film about a small group of people who survive the explosion of an atomic bomb. Using a face-to-face interview technique, he wanted to have these individuals describe the horror of their experiences as they huddled together in a cellar. This film was never made, but Watkins proposed a similar project for his first BBC production. BBC officials, however, suggested that he choose a less controversial subject for his first film. After the success of *Culloden*, he again approached Huw Wheldon about the possibility of making a film on the topic of nuclear warfare. Watkins was now no longer thinking merely in terms of depicting the accounts of a few survivors. His concept had broadened to the point where he proposed that the film deal with most, if not all, of the major wide-ranging consequences of a nuclear attack on England.

Such an endeavor demanded careful documentation, and from November, 1964, through March, 1965, Watkins researched his topic and prepared his script. He talked with a rocket expert about the "Honest John" rocket and discussed the effects of radioactivity with scientists from London University and the London Institute of Strategic Studies. Much of his investigation, however, focused on books that had been rarely seen by the general public. One such work, *The Effects of Nuclear Weapons*, edited by Samuel Glasstone and published by the United States Atomic Energy Commission, supplied a considerable amount of the statistical information cited in the film. Using this material, Watkins constructed what he called a "mathematical pyramid," which applied a kind of mathematical logic to the probable nuclear target areas in England, the projected number of people who would be killed, the probable restrictions that authorities would have to put into operation, and the likely difficulties that would result from a condition of martial law. Since everything in the film is a projection of what might happen in the event of nuclear conflict, the vision offered by the filmmaker is, of necessity, a highly personal one. Yet because of the research and this so-called mathematical pyramid, which employed the most conservative estimates in all categories, Watkins insisted that his film could not be dismissed as a random fantasy.

While books may have been the cornerstone of Watkins' research in technical areas, they played little part in what he called the sociological area.

> The sociological background to a third world war was just as important to me as the technical research, but here the research was more in terms of people than books. I went to see thirty to fifty people, ranging from poets and sculptors to conductors, composers, writers, producers, and so on. I wanted to hear what they felt about the silence on the whole subject of the effect of nuclear war, and what they felt about their part as intellectuals in contributing to the silence. . . . These meetings were the most interesting and moving part of the research, and the responses I obtained were continually fed back into the film.[12]

Such feedback caused Watkins' script to grow to massive proportions, and at times, the detailed information became too much for most potential audiences to absorb. Indeed, the script in this form became impossible to film, and during the four weeks of shooting in April, 1965, Watkins cut out repetitious information, certain dramatic incidents, and even the semblance of a narrative thread which followed key figures, such as the doctor and fire chief, and which provided a more conventional pattern of continuity. Although Watkins made numerous changes in the script because of the contingencies of shooting, at this point in his career he still depended heavily on a detailed script to guide him. Sequences in the final film may give the impression of spontaneous reality, but almost everything in the actual shooting was carefully organized, including, with only a few notable exceptions, even the responses of the people being interviewed. "Yes, I get it all on paper, and then I shoot and it all changes because of special circumstances of weather and people and all sorts of things. But I certainly try to start with a very detailed script, because you can't improvise this sort of thing. It's difficult enough to organize with a working script, but without it would be chaos. You're not working with professional actors, so you've got to organize private people who are coming on their own time and the thing is an immense jigsaw puzzle to work out, to shoot."[13]

Since there were no characters in *The War Game* developed beyond the most basic level, intense work with cast members was limited to one or two scenes of short duration. What mattered most was the cast member's ability to project somewhat complicated emotions as realistically as possible, and to this end, Watkins occasionally even wrote the "uhs" and pauses into their speeches. He then spent a short time setting the context for them, explaining to each person the kind of responses that he desired, and in many cases, even acting it out. The effectiveness of such a method is perhaps most vividly illustrated in *The War Game* by the young woman who portrays a nurse and explains to the camera, as she attempts to hold back her tears, that many of the people she is trying to care for are literally falling apart. Although he exercised considerable control over the responses of his nonprofessionals, Watkins still feels that each individual who worked on the film was allowed to put something of himself into his performance. Speaking specifically of the woman who played the nurse, he says, "I suggested to her that it was a very difficult and emotional moment for her . . . and she did cry. She didn't do it because I was tweaking her foot or jumping up and down in the background. She did it because she felt it. Now obviously I and the circumstances I have created here played a very strong part in obtaining that kind of reaction, as well as what the person himself is giving and feeling and sensing."[14]

One of the notable exceptions in *The War Game* to the rigidly controlled reactions of the cast involved the interviews with townspeople about their knowledge of Strontium 90 and about whether there should be a retaliatory strike if Russia bombed England. The people presented in these interviews had agreed to participate in the film, and many had already been involved in the filming of the fire-storm sequence. They were now separated from the rest of the cast and given the opportunity to answer an interviewer's questions with what they sincerely felt or thought themselves. According to Watkins, ". . . for a moment they became what they really were—ordinary lay members of the British public. I asked these questions about fifty feet away from the main group; no one could hear what I was saying. And those questions and responses—particularly the responses—are perhaps the biggest single indictment in the entire film of the way we are conducting our present society and of the lack of common public knowledge of the things which affect humanity."[15]

Watkins' use of nonprofessionals in *The War Game* in no way breaks from his concern with the communal experience that so clearly marked his amateur film productions and *Culloden*. All of the people involved in the making of the film listened to Watkins speak at meetings about what he hoped to accomplish by making a film on this subject and how the experience of working on this film could affect them. After such general meetings, Watkins then met individually with each of those who expressed a desire to participate, in order "to pull him into the communal thing of making films." According to Watkins, there is no set method to achieve realistic performances from nonprofessional cast members. It is part of a "collective experience which grows from the meetings, the brief individual discussions, and the involvement that comes from working together."[16]

This harmony of working together may have existed among director, cast, and crew, but it did not extend to members of the BBC hierarchy, who were rather tense about this project even before the film was finished. Richard Cawston, who replaced Wheldon as head of Documentary Programmes just as Watkins was about to begin filming *The War Game*, suggests that there were reservations about the project from the beginning:

It was a hell of a difficult subject, involving as it did the national defense policy of the country. It was not a thing on which the BBC could lightly embark. I am sure it's a thing that no other organization in the world would have embarked on at all, but Huw Wheldon wanted to make it possible. Because it was a delicate, difficult subject and because it was likely to undermine the government of the day, and the national defense policy, and NATO, and God knows what, he had to use the normal BBC process which is to refer up to your next senior person to check whether a thing is okay. In this case, it was referred right to the director general of the BBC.... Huw gave it his full support . . . and the agreement reached was that it could be made on the understanding that first the script, and then the completed film, would have to be seen by the director general and, if necessary, by the board of governors. It was on these conditions that Peter was allowed to go ahead with the film, and I think it is very important, in view of the events which followed, that Peter knew that the film . . . would have to be seen at that level before it could be approved for transmission.[17]

The first hint of trouble came even before the filming began when BBC officials told Watkins that he was not going to obtain certain information he had requested from the Home Office and that he should not make trouble by pursuing the matter. Watkins had presented a forty-point questionnaire to the central branch of the Ministry of Civil Defense. Surely some of the questions touched on classified materials, but Watkins claims that about eighty percent of the questions were within areas of knowledge that should have been available to the public. No attempt was made to present unclassified information to the filmmaker; rather it appears that the Home Office made some high-level complaints to the BBC, a practice which is not especially unusual. According to one BBC official, the television corporation continuously receives high-level complaints about its programming from a number of sources.

It is likely that the BBC defended Watkins in this instance, but the government's dismay over this project was illustrated by the fact that the Home Office withdrew all official assistance and ordered other government agencies to do the same, even to the point of refusing to supply uniforms, ambulances, and geiger counters. The only agency which unofficially offered help was the Kent Auxiliary Fire Service; and because of its cooperation, Watkins was able to make the fire-storm sequence one of his most chillingly effective examples of realistic reconstruction.

After four weeks of shooting in April, 1965, Watkins began the three-month process of editing 20,000 feet of film to a rough cut of about 2,000 feet. When the editing was about four-fifths completed, Watkins talked about his film with James Blue and Michael Gill in an interview which was later printed in *Film Comment*. This discussion is rather astonishing because Watkins brashly, but accurately, predicts the situation that arose a few months later when Hugh Carleton Greene, director general of the BBC, viewed the film.

It's not so much that facts are deliberately withheld from people as being a gentlemen's agreement not to tell people – and this is why my film, *The War Game*, will really curl the eyeballs of a lot of higher ups. They will have to decide that it is not right for people to know these things, because "this will affect the war morale of Britain," and that's going to be a hell of a thing to decide. . . . In other words, *is the withholding of knowledge a good thing?* And the only kind of argument they can put forward if they reject the film, is – "You musn't [*sic*] frighten people." And this, I will say, "doesn't wash." And they will have to repeat – "You mustn't frighten," and then we shall really be going to town.[18]

During the editing of *The War Game*, Watkins was especially conscious about not making the film too horrific or too depressing for a television audience. He wanted it to shock, but he felt that in its final form, it did not have the impact of *Culloden*; "it's not as brutal, certainly it's not horrific."[19] This point is reiterated in a January 26, 1966, letter sent to the nearly four hundred cast members of *The War Game* about a cast screening of the film. Watkins mentions that he had originally thought the film would run about ninety minutes, but because of "the consistently depressing nature of the subject," he decided it should not run for more than about fifty minutes.

When Watkins completed his rough cut, he screened it for Huw Wheldon and Richard Cawston. Wheldon was especially disturbed by sequences involving actions of the police in the film. He was not happy with a scene in which police officers were murdered by townspeople in Kent, but he more strongly criticized two other sequences as errors in judgment. He objected to the depiction of policemen relieving the misery of dying people in the forward medical aid stations and to the presentation of police summarily executing rioters, under Article 17 of the National Emergency Code. Wheldon argued that these duties would have been performed by the army, since in England, the police are seen as being on the side of the public. Watkins, much to the consternation of his superiors, refused to alter these sequences, since part of his intention was to show the breakdown of traditional modes of behavior which might result from a nuclear attack. He did

172460

agree to a number of other changes, including the insertion of such captions as "based on the statements of an Anglican bishop," in order to make sure the audience understood that it was watching a reconstructed interview rather than an actual event. The hypothetical nature of the film was also underscored by the narrator who continually used such phrases as "it is probable that . . ." and "there would possibly be no alternative." Finally, to make sure that no one in the audience could possibly confuse reconstruction with reality, Richard Cawston proposed to insert a disclaimer at the beginning of the film indicating that what followed was one man's view of what might happen in the event of a nuclear attack. These changes, the already existing role of the narrator in the film, and Cawston's proposal are important in light of the arguments later used by top BBC officials to justify the banning of the film.

Originally, *The War Game* was scheduled for transmission during the week of August 6, 1965, the twentieth anniversary of the bombing of Hiroshima, but by late July, it had been postponed indefinitely. From our present perspective, it is difficult to gauge the impact and extent of the controversy surrounding the banning of this film, but a careful examination of the extensive material found in the British press from September, 1965, through May, 1966, indicates that the BBC action had considerable ramifications.

In early September, 1965, a civil defense officer who had provided some technical advice to *The War Game* crew announced that the screening of the film would have "a terrible effect on public morale." Almost immediately after this comment was printed, Mary Whitehouse, cofounder of the Clean-up TV Campaign, wrote to Prime Minister Wilson and to Conservative leader Edward Heath. Both assured Mrs. Whitehouse that "decisions on matters of this kind are made at the highest level in the BBC after appropriate consultations and take full account of public policy."

By late November, it became public that on September 2, Lord Normanbrook, chairman of the BBC board of governors, had seen the film and declared that it must be previewed by representatives of the government before it could be decided to transmit the program. On September 24, various government people, including representatives from the Home Office, saw the film and supposedly pointed out "inaccuracies" and advised against telecasting the film.

On November 26, four days after this information appeared in British newspapers and two days after two Labor members of Parliament came to question him about the film and about pressure from the Home Office, Sir Hugh Greene announced that *The War Game* would not be shown because "it was too horrific for the medium of broadcasting." He also emphasized that the BBC made its own decision without any "outside pressure of any kind."

Published reports indicated that Greene felt the film would frighten people in the same way that Orson Welles' radio braodcast of *The War of the Worlds* alarmed some Americans in 1938. Such a comparison was both unfortunate and unfair. Welles' program was a conscious hoax in which simulated newscasts were intended to be misconstrued as real. Watkins' film was a serious work, and while its newsreellike realism was meant to jolt viewers, *The War Game* never attempted to hoodwink the audience into believing that what it was seeing was anything more than a possible consequence of nuclear war. Welles intended his program as a Halloween joke; the purpose of Watkins' film was "to break the silence on the subject . . . and to evoke sufficient public discussion to enlarge the whole issue . . . and to try and provoke people, to involve people to political or social or media means of confrontation."[20]

The major discussions that the film initially provoked, however, all related to the topic of censorship. Although Wheldon and Cawston supported the showing of the film, they were prepared to accept Greene's decision. Watkins, on the other hand, was not. In September, 1965, he had resigned, in part because of the BBC response to his film, and then he took the unprecedented and ungentlemanly step, in the words of one official, "of declaring war on the BBC." He began a concerted campaign to save the film by writing countless letters to newspapers, university professors, and cinema clubs, and probably it was only through his persistent efforts that the film was ever shown to the public.

From the beginning, Watkins insisted that the decision not to show the film was the result of pressure placed on the BBC by the Home Office, and the fact that the BBC admitted that

Home Office officials saw the film at a private screening certainly gave credence to this position. To this day, however, the
BBC claims that the banning of the film "was not a political
decision. It had nothing to do with the fact that the film was
anti-government. The BBC is not worried by government. We
are very independent." Still, the interest that government
spokesmen took in this film was nothing short of extraordinary. Even after the British Film Institute took over the
cinema distribution of the film, the Foreign Office fought
against allowing it to be the official entry for the tele-documen-
tary section of the 1966 Venice Festival. A letter written to
Watkins by a senior officer of the Institute at this time states
that "it is perhaps worth mentioning that the arguments
against the film topped all in ultimate absurdity. The principal
one was that it would be quite impossible for foreigners to
identify themselves with such a curiously English location as
Kent. They would tend to think that what they saw on the
screen was not what might happen in any society subject to
nuclear bombing, but a curious quirk of the English. How daft
can you get?"

In any case, no matter what the real reasons were for refusing to telecast *The War Game*, the BBC attempted to defend its
decision in rather suspect ways. Watkins was told by one of his
superiors that the film was "less than a masterpiece." Indeed,
if this were part of the criteria for telecasting films at the BBC,
the tube would remain blank 364 days a year. A form reply was
also sent by the BBC to those individuals and organizations
who wrote letters seeking reasons behind the decision not to
show the film. This form letter stated that the BBC undertook
to make the film because "it recognizes the possibility of nuclear attack raises matters of public concern." It also suggested
that there was an "element of experiment" in the production
which was unsuccessful. "Such programme experiments
sometimes fail and have to be put on one side at some stage in
production, even though money has been spent on them." In
the last sentence of the letter, this reasoning was then con-
tradicted by the admission that *The War Game* was a film of
"great merit." The bulk of the BBC argument, however, focused on the view that

the horror of the film was . . . of an entirely different quality to that
which is contained in the recognisably fictional presentations of

some television films. It was also different in its impact from the objective presentation of past horrors – such as scenes which might be shown in documentaries on Culloden, the Hiroshima bombings or the extermination of the Warsaw Ghetto. Such scenes, because of their fictional character or because of their historic setting, do not have the personal application . . . of *The War Game*, which conveys the sense that what it is showing could happen to people who might be watching it.

As such, "the BBC has therefore reluctantly decided that, because of its nature, this film cannot be broadcast. No matter how late at night it was screened, and whatever warnings might be given before the showing, we could not be certain that the audience would not include some for whom its horrors would have reached the point of danger."[21]

During this period of controversy, BBC officials also began describing the film with such phrases as "without hope" and "lacking in human warmth." These attitudes, in part, grew out of the fact that Watkins did not depict the resilience of the English character; he did not show Britons acting with the same spirit they exhibited during the London blitz.

The cruelest attack of all, however, was not on the film, but on the man himself. In "Why They Made *The War Game*," a feature story in the *Sunday Telegraph* of February 13, 1966, Grace Wyndham Goldie, a former talk show and current affairs head at the BBC, claimed that Watkins himself had told her that he used trip wires and starvation tactics to elicit the convincing performances from his amateur actors in *Culloden*. Felix Aylmer, president of British Actor's Equity, immediately joined in the attack against Watkins' use of amateurs in his films and his supposed inhumane treatment of them. Watkins' passionate denials were immediately supported by Derek Ware, who served as battle coordinator for *Culloden*, and by numerous letters from cast members to various newspapers. Still, a BBC official publicly stated that Watkins' denial should not be interpreted to reflect the corporation's view. Watkins immediately demanded a retraction and an apology and received them both in the next televised BBC newscast.

Finally, as a means of gaining support for his decision, Hugh Greene arranged two private screenings of *The War Game* at the National Film Theatre, for invited guests only. These guests were limited to rather carefully defined categories, which included members of Parliament, members of the Home Office, military officers, people from the British film industry, and members of the press, especially defense and political commentators. In a letter to a Labor member of Parliament, one of the highest BBC officials made it quite clear that he regarded "this list as representing the limit of our obligation. . . . I do not see that the BBC ought to make this film available to audiences other than those we are now inviting." As such, the general public and even critics, such as the editor of *Sight and Sound* and the television columnist for the *Evening Standard*, were kept out. Anthony Shrimsley, political analyst for *The Daily Mirror*, suggested that all of this was done so that Greene could get a "political blessing" for his decision (which he did). For Shrimsley, however, the BBC was playing a dangerous censorship game which might ultimately backfire and limit its freedom in the future.[22]

The BBC even went so far as to suggest that these screenings were being held as a "kind of tribute" to Watkins, and presumably it was during the introductory comments to one of them that Kenneth Adam, director of the BBC, defied logic by remarking, "I am sure that Peter Watkins would be the first to agree that the greatest compliment that we can pay him is not to show his film."[23]

In a 1977 letter to the author about *The War Game* controversy, Kenneth Adam expressed dismay that someone was "reviving these old sores," but he did indicate that for the BBC, "the essential distinction to be made is between an involuntary audience and a voluntary one. That is why having taken the decision not to show the film on television, I then made it available to the British Film Institute, of which I was at the time a Governor, and gave them world rights. . . . And, a great many more people in the last resort have seen it, I have no doubt, than people would have done if I had agreed to its being shown on television."[24]

The official decision to ban *The War Game* was made by Hugh Greene and not by Kenneth Adam, and Adam's view here suggests that the BBC was anxious to have the film seen in cinemas even though it could not be seen on British television. This, however, was not the case. The decision to allow the film to be shown by the British Film Institute came about only after considerable pressure from members of Parliament and the press, and after Watkins published a number of letters in various newspapers. These letters detailed his proposals to purchase the film outright, his failed attempts to get the BBC to release the film to cinemas, and his intention to remake *The War Game* as a feature film. As late as January 28, 1966, a high BBC official made it quite clear, in a letter to a Labor M.P., that he did "not propose to make the film available for circulation to film societies" and that he had "no present intention of seeking . . . rights" which would allow the film to be seen theatrically or by film societies. Finally, in March, 1966, the BBC announced that the film would be shown at the BFI's National Film Theatre in London and would then be released to cinemas throughout the country. The film was also given a commercial cinema release in Europe and America and went on to win an Academy Award for the Best Documentary of 1966. The BBC, however, refused to allow interested television networks in Sweden, West Germany, France, and Canada to telecast the film, and the world-wide ban on television screenings of the film is still in effect today. In July, 1977, Richard Cawston indicated that he and Alastair Mill had discussed a review of the ban and even the possibility of showing the film on the BBC, in "the light of the change in public acceptability." Not only has nothing come from this proposal, but in May, 1978, the BBC refused to grant a Swedish television channel permission to show a short excerpt from the film in the context of a program devoted to nuclear issues. In January, 1979, when Cecila Zadig, producer of this Swedish television program, again checked with BBC officials about the proposed review of the ban on *The War Game*, she was told that there was no change in the BBC position.

Until the BBC archive files on *The War Game* are made public, it remains almost impossible to determine the exact reasons for the banning of this film. Aside from the political issues, the "horrific" film position, the voluntary-involuntary audience concept, and the claim that the artistic merits of the film were not great enough to offset the arguments used against its screening, one suspects that the BBC philosophy of "objectivity" played some role in this decision. In fact, the most significant aspect of the entire controversy may very well be the clash between "subjective" and "objective" theories of documentary filmmaking.

In the early sixties, Ken Russell broke down some of the restrictions imposed by the BBC on the use of actors to impersonate people who had actually lived, but sequences from some of his *Monitor* films were trimmed or cut because of the BBC's "established" views of documentary. Huw Wheldon, for instance, objected to a sequence in *Elgar* (1962) in which Russell juxtaposed sections of the "Pomp and Circumstance March" to gruesome World War I newsreel footage, because the attitude was attributed to Elgar with Russell "speaking on his behalf." By 1966, however, concepts of objectivity broadened, and in the BBC letter about the cancellation of *The War Game*, even *Culloden* was described as an "objective presentation of past horrors."

In a 1977 interview with the author, Richard Cawston elaborated on the BBC concern with objectivity. "I think everybody is a personal filmmaker, but I think that you have to separate the business of objectivity between what we call subjects of high public concern, that is to say really political subject matter on the one hand, and almost everything else on the other. . . . Our attitude about objectivity only occurs in that political arena because we have so few channels in this country. . . . There is not enough alternative editorializing for the audience to select." These views are further amplified in *Principles and Practice in Documentary Programmes*, a BBC pamphlet chiefly written by Cawston. Here Cawston argues that if a producer / director expresses his views on "matters of high controversy" in a program, he is abusing the platform he controls. The director, of course, must be given complete freedom to select his camera angles, music, lenses, and editing style, but in making a film on a "subject of high public concern," he must "subordinate his own particular bias . . . and use these devices solely to add clarity and illumination and meaning, and not to add another opinion to the programme." The reason why a filmmaker must be prevented from expression of his own personal contentions "is simply that audiences have come to accept BBC programmes as the work of the BBC—part of its continuous flow. Even though a programme may be clearly labelled with the name of its producer or director, the great mass of the viewing public will believe that it has been produced in accordance with the BBC's generally recognised codes of fairness and balance, and this is a belief to be cherished."[25]

For Cawston and a number of detractors, *The War Game* was considered a "tract" for nuclear disarmament and Watkins "a missionary" whose allegiance to the Campaign for Nuclear Disarmament perverted and distorted the presentation of his information. While Watkins may have been sympathetic with many of the aims of the CND, he was never directly associated with it and had numerous reservations about the tactics of this particular organization. In any case, Watkins in no way considered the film as a "tract" for the CND.[26]

At this point in his life, Watkins seemed unresolved about the nature of documentary in particular and television in general. This ambivalence is noticeable if one carefully examines his 1965 interview with James Blue and Michael Gill. On the one hand, he seems to have accepted the BBC's doctrine of balance and fairness to the extent that he genuinely sees his film as an attempt to counteract the silence that existed in media about this issue. Thus the film itself, in Watkins' view, is a balancing force. He also talks about "the truth" of the film and even suggests that lots of people who see it may even decide that "the thermonuclear posture" is a necessary thing in order to prevent the holocaust depicted in the film, "At least that person can say that with some knowledge now, because formerly when anyone put a cross on a ballot-sheet, it was without any knowledge at all." A page later, however, Watkins indicates that the film was something of a "cheat": "You could say that it is life as Peter Watkins sees it, and yet in a way it isn't, because I've never seen an atomic attack." Watkins then goes on to discuss the logic of how he went from the premise of believing an antinuclear film was necessary to the view that a nuclear war would result in a civil defense collapse and how he set out to prove it. His focus at this point and for most of the remainder of the interview involves a totally subjective perspective.

If nothing else, the controversy over *The War Game* forced Watkins to examine further his ideas about the nature of documentary and the role of the media in today's world, and, in a number of ways, *Privilege* can be seen as his response to the "subjective-objective" debate. Before discussing *Privilege*, however, it is necessary, now that the proper context has been established, to analyze briefly the achievements and failures of *The War Game*.

Although Watkins cut much material from his original shoot-

ing script of *The War Game*, his final version is a carefully
structured work, which like *Culloden*, depends for its impact
on counterpoint editing techniques and shifting time perspectives. In *Culloden*, the narrator constantly forced the viewer to
realize connections between the past and the present; in *The
War Game*, the editing impels the viewer to see how the logic
of the present may lead to the events of the future. Both films
exhibit what Watkins calls a "block structure." While he used
this organizational pattern more widely in *The War Game*, he
feels that he did so less satisfactorily because of time pressures
in the editing stages of the film. Still, the major impact of the
film is intimately linked to this structure which juxtaposed the
strategies of the present with the supposed "fantasy" of the
possible future. Since Watkins felt that the possibilities of nuclear war were much closer to reality than to fantasy, he sub-
verted the traditional present-future approach by making the
policy statements of the present appear to be the improbable
fantasy element in his film and the possible future of a nuclear
attack the stark reality. It is crucial to understand this shift in
order to realize how the film works. Obviously Hugh Greene
and other BBC officials failed to do so, or they could never
have compared Watkins' film to Orson Welles' radio broadcast
of *The War of the Worlds*.

Both the strength and the weaknesses of *The War Game* derive, for the most part, from this unusual reversal of "fantasy"
and "reality" and the counterpointing of them. The reality of
the future is underscored by newsreellike techniques which
Watkins had already successfully employed in previous films.
The fantasy element of present-day opinions about the aftermath of a nuclear attack is reinforced by the artificiality of the
interview situations, the "canned" atmosphere surrounding
these commentators, and the use of printed captions and quotations.

Contrary to the claims of critics who argue that Watkins
sought to eliminate all distancing conventions through his reconstruction techniques, the frequent use of printed material
and the commentators (called "interrupters" by Watkins in a
letter to cast members) establishes an almost Brechtian sense
of detachment. These devices constantly remind the viewer
that he is watching a film. In a paradoxical way, however, Watkins' use of this material increases the emotional impact of the

A production still from *The War Game*.

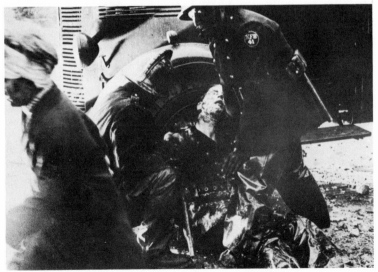

The War Game –from the fire storm sequence.

film. Through counterpoint editing, the inadequacies and ab-
surdities of statements dealing with aspects of nuclear war are
presented against the "actuality" of a nuclear attack. Watkins
is obviously conscious of the power of the image over the
word, and what emerges is not so much a dialectical structure
pitting word against image, as the demolition of a particular
rationale for a position on the use of nuclear weapons. Watkins
is not presenting a balanced debate; he is destroying the
"logic" of a position which deals with people as mere statistics
and which has not presented realistic facts to the public. In a
number of interviews in 1965 and 1966, Watkins acknowledged that there might be something in the balance-of-power
argument for nuclear weapons, but not in the overkill stage
that presently existed. A viewer might come to the belief that a
policy of nuclear deterrents is necessary after viewing *The
War Game*, but presumably this person would not use the
logic offered by the interrupters in the film. Thus, while *The
War Game* is structured to affect the viewer and to move him
in an emotional manner, Watkins, unlike Joseph Goebbels,
never intended *The War Game* or any of his work "to destroy
people's internal psyche . . . or to zap people so thoroughly
that they were left with no thinking faculties themselves."[27]

The major problem with Watkins' structure in *The War
Game* stems from the artificial presentation of the interrupters
in the context of the graphic realism of everything else in the
film. For instance, while available lighting and a fast film
stock were used for the reconstructed action, the interrupters
seem to be filmed with a conventional, theatrical lighting
scheme. The framing of the interrupters is much more traditional than anywhere else in the film, and even the *mise-
en-scène* (book cases, office desks, and a blackboard) for these
sequences seems contrived. None of the interrupters is ever
identified by name, and few are even designated by occupa-
tion. The audience simply encounters the faces of individuals
who, for the most part, utter preposterous projections. Finally,
the nonprofessional actors portraying the nuclear strategist,
the bishop, and the psychologist lack the convincing qualities
demonstrated by the amateur actors elsewhere in the film.
Perhaps Watkins wanted this effect in order to increase the
irony and the improbability of the arguments offered by these
individuals, and certainly the crosscutting of the American

nuclear strategist and the Anglican bishop with the fire-storm sequences is devastatingly effective. Still, the contrast seems too extreme. Even though every opinion spoken by an inter-rupter is taken from the actual statements of living people, for some viewers it is not the credibility of the arguments that is called into question but the fact that these arguments actually represent mainstream establishment positions. The most no-table example is the nuclear strategist, who indicates he be-lieves that in the next world war, "both sides could stop before the ultimate destruction of cities, so that both sides could re-tire for a period of ten years or so of post-attack recuperation, in which world wars IV to VIII could be prepared." The chil-ling effect of these words, when spoken by an awkward-look-ing man with disheveled hair and a strangely trimmed beard, is lessened because of the man's physical appearance. What the film does not tell the viewer is that these utterances were drawn from statements made by the nuclear strategist Herman Kahn. Indeed, any cursory reading of *On Thermonuclear War* or "Thirty-Eight Rungs to Spasm—Or Insensitive Wars" will illustrate that many of the interrupters' remarks in *The War Game* are not only accurate but are also representative of in-fluential attitudes in the early sixties.

If the artificiality of the interrupters casts doubt on the ac-ceptance of their views as representative of the establishment, Watkins' depiction of the effects of a nuclear attack contains no lapse in credibility. The technical aspects (Lilias Munro's makeup, Peter Bartlett's photography, Derek Ware's stunt work, etc.), convincing performances by amateurs, and Wat-kins' newsreellike techniques combine to present a chilling portrayal of the director's vision of the possible, perhaps even probable, future.

It is not enough simply to say that Watkins carried forward his methods of filmmaking from *Culloden* to *The War Game*. In subtle ways, he advanced his techniques. His handling of crowd sequences in *The War Game* is far more sophisticated than in *Culloden*, where a sharp eye can distinguish the same actor playing a number of different roles. Watkins also uses some individuals for multiple roles in his nuclear film, but here it is almost impossible to locate them. The newsreel ap-proach is effectively employed in both films, but in the fire-storm sequence, through zooms, rapid pans, and the jostling of the camera, Watkins achieves a level of realism hitherto unattained in his work. In *Culloden*, Watkins utilizes both the long take and the freeze frame. In *The War Game*, his long takes also become masterful tracking shots, such as the opening shot of a motorcycle policeman delivering a message to a regional committee meeting and the later sequence depicting Dr. David Thornley's visit to a patient just before the explosion of an off-target nuclear missile. Watkins employs numerous freeze frames, which when considered in conjunction with the long takes establish a rhythm that reflects the pattern of the block structure which dominates the first half of the film. *The War Game* even extends Watkins' experiments with sound. Like *Culloden*, there is no nonsynchronous music to heighten the dramatic impact, but at a few points in the film, he mixes together two tracks—one of synchronous sound and one with sounds from previous sequences. Thus when British citizens are being interviewed about buying supplies to build a bomb shelter in their homes, sirens blare in the background to generate tension. The same device is repeated later when undercurrents of moaning punctuate interviews and scenes of

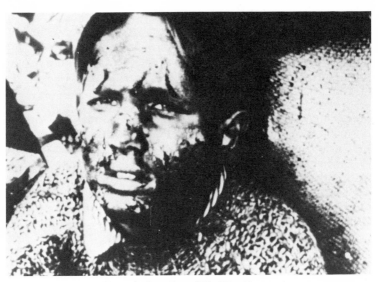

From the last shot of *The War Game*.

policemen killing those placed in category 3 at forward medical aid centers. These experiments with nonsynchronous sound are minor at best, but they are the first steps toward the complex sound montages, which, in *Punishment Park* and *Edvard Munch*, become as important, if not more so, than visual montage.

The use of the narrator remains the one area in which *The War Game* does not really make advances over *Culloden*. In *Culloden*, the narrator functions on a variety of levels and is instrumental in shifting the perspectives of the audience. In *The War Game*, Watkins uses two narrators: one voice for presenting the passage of events in newsreel fashion, and the other for detailing statistics and the probable effects of radioactivity, etc. Out of necessity, this second voice often speaks in conditional clauses, and as such, he lacks the authority of the narrator in *Culloden*. It appears that Watkins may have been conscious of this loss. Rather than serving as a narrator himself, he used voices which for British viewers had authority and the "chill of authenticity." Michael Aspel, a well-known BBC television news reader, supplied one voice, and Dick Graham, who often did documentary commentaries, the other.

Like the narrator of *The Forgotten Faces* and *Culloden*, Dick Graham, near the end of the film, succinctly summarizes the major theme—a theme which has already been elucidated by the film's structure.

On almost the entire subject of thermonuclear weapons, on the problems of their possession, on the effects of their use, there is now practically a total silence in the press, in official publications, and on television. There is hope in any unresolved and unpredictable situation, but is there a real hope to be found in this silence? The world's stockpile of thermonuclear weapons has doubled in the last five years and now is the equivalent of almost 20 tons of high explosives to every man, woman and child on the planet. This stockpile is still steadily growing.

The War Game has not lost its effectiveness in the last fourteen years. It remains Watkins' most widely screened film, and although some of the factual information has become dated, its emotional impact has not, even though too many of us have learned to live with the threat of the bomb. If there is a change today, it is perhaps most notably found in the attitudes of some of those who might serve as present-day equivalents to the interrupters in *The War Game*. For instance, Colonel Gerald Patterson, a Canadian Force Officer attached to NORAD Headquarters, claims that "the Soviets are getting bigger and better every day. They are building the biggest military machine in history. There are two things that bother the hell out of me. First is that the Soviets have never abided by any treaty that didn't satisfy them, and the second is that there has never been a military machine built that wasn't used, not ever. Is this the sudden exception?"[28] Indeed, it is difficult to call Watkins' vision paranoid anymore when even military experts agree that the possibility of nuclear war seems dangerously close to probability before the end of the century.

3

The Metaphorical Features: *Privilege,* *The Gladiators* and *Punishment Park*

THE WAR GAME controversy had an enormous impact on Peter Watkins and on the development of his career. Certainly, the publicity surrounding the film and its director played a key role in getting Jay Kanter, Universal Studio's European production head, to include Watkins in his plans to employ young, gifted European filmmakers for a series of low and moderately budgeted productions. Even more significant, however, is the role that the controversy played in shaping Watkins' attitudes toward the media and his role in them. In less than a year, he experienced a meteoric rise and fall within the hallowed halls of the BBC. He quickly went from being considered "the most talented new director working in television" to being considered an immature troublemaker who ignored his responsibilities as a television director. Watkins claims that while he could handle the shift in attitude on the part of the BBC top brass, he was totally unprepared for the reaction of his peers:

I used to get very much attacked by some of my colleagues for having made the film ... producers and directors in the BBC and elsewhere coming up and really making the most unpleasant personal remarks at me because I had made *The War Game*. ... It caused many of my own group, my own professional colleagues within the BBC, to do the very difficult thing of trying to decide whether or not they would support me—and, of course, most of them didn't. A few wrote me letters ... saying they did support me but they couldn't speak out publicly about it. Many I think decided not to support me; some said I would drive people to suicide; others were angry with me; others were probably angry with themselves for not having supported me. I am guessing here, but I think it is not an inaccurate guess.[1]

69

Indeed, in a letter to Watkins dated February 10, 1966, a "friend" and established documentary producer claimed that he heard that a BBC department head "thought that 10,000 people would attempt to take their own lives" if the film was televised. The writer of the letter suggests that this view is a bit extreme, but then goes on to add: "The probability would be, I fear, that there would be perhaps a dozen suicides on [sic] a nationwide showing. . . . Would you feel guilty if, after a TV showing, a dozen suicides were reported? It is a question you must face." Suggestions such as this one that he was ignoring his responsibility as a programmaker forced Watkins to reevaluate the BBC's attitudes toward the viewing public and responsibility in broadcasting. For him, the case history of *The War Game* served as a severe indictment of television's arrogance toward, and contempt for, its viewing audience. The attacks on *The War Game* for presenting a biased view to an audience presumably unable to find alternative viewpoints stemmed from the belief that it was not only possible but necessary to pursue the goal of objectivity. Watkins, who never lost sight of the role of personal expression in his work, now not only defended the integrity of personal filmmaking, but began to express doubts that anything "objective," in the BBC sense of the word, could ever be attained. As such, *The War Game*, which purports to be Watkins' vision of what might happen if a nuclear attack were launched against Great Britain, is much less dangerous than television documentaries and newscasts which under the guise of objectivity, editorialize often through the subtle combining of "the pseudo-objective quality of photo-movement with the direct exposition of unphotographable realities."[2] For Watkins, the responsibilities of media begin with a recognition that the "realities" they present are, in fact, subjective "realities."

At this point in time, Watkins felt that the only way to counter what he perceived to be the adverse effects of media manipulation was to make a "strong personal propaganda film." His first two professional films had opened a new vista in documentary film style, and with *Privilege*, he would extend even further a method of filmmaking which raises serious questions about traditional documentary form. Watkins now suggests that it is difficult for him to determine the degree to which he consciously intended at that time to create films which would subvert traditional documentary form. Certainly, however, this is one of the effects of his experiments with merging metaphorical and documentary techniques in *Privilege*, *The Gladiators*, and *Punishment Park*, films which critic Raymond Durgnat aptly calls "society fiction," not science fiction.

Privilege

The idea for *Privilege* is said to have come from a conversation between Terence Stamp and John Heyman, a former agent turned producer. Stamp suggested "making a film of a pop singer who thought he was Jesus Christ." Heyman replied: "I thought they all do." From these casual remarks grew the idea for a story which would "expose the rotten world of pop."[3] John Speight, creator of the British television series *Till Death Us Do Part*, which later served as the basis for *All in the Family*, wrote the original story. Norman Bogner, an American novelist, whose works included *Divorce* and *Spanish Fever*, then turned the story into his first screenplay. Once Bogner had finished a script which satirically attacked the pop world's unscrupulous use of power and the manipulation of popular taste, Heyman approached Peter Watkins about directing the film. Watkins accepted and worked closely with Bogner in revising the script. The conventional narrative development was altered to fit Watkins' proposed approach of fusing metaphor with realistic interview techniques. Also, the focus was sharpened on the theme of the establishment and media joining forces to divert people from serious consideration of the problems of our society.

In its final form, the shooting script depicts Britain in the near future. The country's most successful pop entertainer, Steven Shorter, with the active support of a coalition government, engages in a violent theatrical rock act which provides his audience with a cathartic release "from the nervous tension caused by the state of the world outside." Young people are thus diverted from politics, and after Steve's appeal reaches the level of hero worship, he is manipulated by church and state into leading the youth of the nation into a "fruitful conformity." At an elaborately staged rally on the first night of Christian Crusade Week, the newly "converted" pop

singer entices nearly fifty thousand people to give themselves
to God and flag. Through the support of Vanessa Ritchie, an
artist commissioned to paint his portrait, Steve finally comes
to express misgivings about his role, and, at an awards presentation, he lashes out at his manipulators and the public at
large. The members of the public, however, have learned their
lessons only too well, and they quickly turn against the man
who was once their idol. The film ends with the narrator ironically commenting that "it's going to be a happy year in Britain
this year in the near future."

Clearly, Watkins' experiences with the BBC played a major
part in some of the reshaping of Bogner's script, but it must not
be interpreted that he forced his views on a reluctant script
writer and producer. Both Bogner and Heyman saw the film as
a sociological work which dealt with various forms of exploita-
tion of both the public and the pop performer.

Privilege remains the highest budgeted Watkins film to date
(roughly about 700,000 dollars), yet it was one of the lowest
budgeted films of the thirteen films that Universal financed in
Britain between 1967 and 1970. It was also Watkins' first color
film, and one of the two films that he shot in 35 mm. The use of
35 mm and a large film crew hampered, to some degree, the
freedom he was accustomed to having as an amateur and BBC
director, and his concern with bounce lighting and using color
in nontheatrical ways demanded constant experimentation
and cooperation from Peter Suschitzky, who served as director
of photography.

Union regulations and working through a casting director
made the use of professional actors a necessity, but Watkins
still managed to secure some nonprofessional actors for the
film, including pop singer Paul Jones and model Jean Shrimpton who played the lead roles. Mark London, who
wrote some of the songs in the film and was originally hired as
technical advisor, found himself portraying Alvin Kirsch, Steven Shorter's press officer. Also, veteran vaudevillian Max Ba-
con, whose previous film experience included a similar role in
Tony Richardson's *The Entertainer*, was asked to play Uncle
Julie. For most of the other supporting roles, Watkins chose
professional actors whose faces were not known to film audiences. Surprisingly enough, the mixture of amateur actors and
professionals is not obvious in the film, and rather than hin-

dering his usual approach, this experience allowed him to extend his use of improvisation beyond anything that had been tried in his previous films. Although a detailed script existed for *Privilege*, certain exchanges and even entire scenes were improvised or worked out by the actors after much discussion with Watkins. Mark London was especially gifted in this area, and such memorable lines as "I would like to introduce your friend, my friend and certainly God's friend, a honey of a chap and a million laughs – Let's welcome the Bishop of Essex" were improvised on the spot.

Watkins also managed to bring to *Privilege* some of the people who had worked with him on previous films: Vanessa Clarke had served as costume designer for *The War Game*; stuntman Derek Ware had coordinated the action sequences in both *Culloden* and *The War Game*, and editor John Trumper had taught Watkins the techniques of editing when the director was a mere assistant editor at World-wide Pictures.

Universal gave Watkins complete freedom to make *Privilege* in the way he intended, and shooting began in Birmingham, England in August, 1966. The film was premiered at the Warner Leicester Square Theatre in London, on April 27, 1967; and from the first screening, it generated controversy. Within the film industry itself, the film was dismissed as representing "the cult of the amateur." Also, at this time, Universal was tied to the Rank organization, and Rank refused to give this "unusual" and "problematic" film a general circuit booking. According to film critic Alexander Walker, this situation existed because "*Privilege* was regarded by a film industry chief with the power to determine its exhibition, as an immoral and un-Christian picture which mocked the Church, defied authority and encouraged youth in lewd practices."[4]

To make matters worse for Watkins, many British critics tended to miss the main thrust of the film's attack and to see it as a misguided satirical assault on the pop world or on the church. The film was castigated by *The Evening Standard* as "a flailing, hysterical, misdirected film," and in a *Times* review entitled "Poor Film From Peter Watkins," John Russell Taylor claimed that this "silly" and "juvenile" film pinned "all on its up-to-the-minute comment on the swinging pop scene." The notable exception to these responses was Penelope Gilliatt, who, in her *Observer* review, claimed that

Privilege was a "brilliant" film which asked questions that politicians should ask but never actually do:

How are we to live? What is the quality of life in metropolitan England now, and what is it going to be in a few years' time? What is the effect of the constant eyewash from publicists and pundits, of modern office buildings, paper clothes, fads whizzing in and out, the use of celebrities as fall-guys, the ethic that celebrates thinking big and ruthlessness, and writes off constancy and compunction? The psychic results shown in the film are a long way towards hell: paranoia, persecution complexes, fawning, suspiciousness, hysteria, a shrinking capacity to inspect ideas, and a more and more generalised emotionalism.[5]

Possibly *Privilege* disappointed its initial audiences almost as much as it displeased the critics. One suspects that the so-called youth audience felt somewhat cheated because the film was not like Richard Lester's films with the Beatles, nor was it even a pop musical in the Cliff Richard fashion, and it made no concessions to those expecting conventional narrative development. On the other hand, those familiar with Watkins' work who went to see the film anticipating the same relentless intensity of *Culloden* and *The War Game* had to adjust to an entirely different pacing, to more traditional camera dynamics, and to a more amorphous filmic structure. Watkins did not entirely dismiss counterpoint editing in *Privilege*, but he subordinated it to other techniques of eliciting tension and of establishing visual rhythms. The camerawork is somewhat fluid but is much less so than what he achieved in his television films; and while the interview method is still employed here, the framing of faces associated with it is often replaced by the more traditional bust shot. These changes probably resulted because of the movement from 16 to 35 mm and the shift from subject matter emphasizing physical suppression to a film depicting psychological subjection and manipulation.

These changes do not mean that *Privilege* should be considered Watkins' most conventional work. Quite the contrary, the film is highly experimental, even beyond Watkins' attempt to fuse realistic techniques to a metaphorical framework. The commentator, for instance, who is used sparingly in *Privilege*, pushes beyond the limitations of the narrator in *The War Game*. Whereas the narrator in *The War Game* spoke about the future with limited authority in conditional clauses, the commentator in *Privilege* (Watkins himself) speaks to the audience with complete knowledge of the future as if it were the present. His role then is not simply to provide background information, character identification and description, and some sense of chronology; rather he underscores the idea that the future depicted in the film is a metaphor for the present. Why this was not obvious to all when the film was released is difficult to understand, especially since some of the so-called prophetic elements in the film were happening almost simultaneously. Violence in rock acts existed at that time in the form of The Who's elaborate smashing of guitars on stage, an activity which probably spawned the dramatic and violent acts of Alice Cooper and Kiss in the seventies. The power and influence of rock personalities were also recognized by establishment representatives of the period. A mere four months after the film was released, Mick Jagger flew via helicopter, from an appeals court in London after a hearing which dismissed his drug sentence, to a plush country estate. Here he engaged in a serious discussion about the state of the world with a group of British notables, including the editor of *The Times*, a former home secretary, the bishop of Woolwich, and Malcolm Muggeridge. Finally, the links between religion and popular music became solidified in the late sixties with the so-called Jesus rock movement. Cliff Richard began to sing for Christ, and even Malcolm Muggeridge mixed religion and popular music in his Trafalgar Square rally of the Crusade for Greater Light.

Since the early 1970s, *Privilege* has enjoyed something of a cult status on the 16 mm nontheatrical college market in the United States, and one suspects that the accuracy with which Watkins presented the directions of rock music has something to do with its popularity. *Privilege*, however, should not be evaluated, even on a superficial level, by the accurate prediction of passing fads. Such a criterion ignores the major concerns of the film and expects a literal working out of all of the film's metaphorical dimensions.

Watkins did not come to *Privilege* with an insider's understanding of the pop world. He depended heavily on *Lonely Boy*, the Canadian Film Board's 1962 *cinéma vérité* documentary on Paul Anka, directed by Wolf Koenig and Ramon Kroitor, to provide him with some insight into the behind-the-scenes world of pop entertainment. Watkins spent days studying photographs of the Hungarian Revolution in preparation for the making of *The Forgotten Faces*, and before beginning work on *Privilege*, he studied *Lonely Boy*, practically frame by frame. As such, this short film infuses *Privilege* from beginning to end. Some people might suggest that Watkins "borrows" too much from *Lonely Boy*, but perhaps it is more accurate to suggest that he "reconstructs" his pop world from the "facts" presented in this film. For instance, Uncle Julie and Alvin Kirsch are obviously modeled on "Uncle" Jules Fidel, owner of the Copacabana, and Irving Feldman, Anka's personal manager. Key lines spoken by Feldman ("Paul, you no longer belong to yourself. You belong to the world") are taken over, slightly altered, and employed in a different context by Alvin Kirsch in talking about Steve Shorter. Also, unintentionally humorous sequences from this Canadian film, such as Anka's presentation of a photograph of himself to Jules Fidel and the thank you kiss in return, are incorporated into *Privilege*, as are mannerisms, the massaging of Paul's neck, and elements of Anka's act. The girl, for instance, who is allowed on stage during Anka's rendition of "Put Your Head on My Shoulder" has a counterpart in the girl who is lowered to the stage during Shorter's "Free Me" number.

Watkins' conception of the nationalistic demonstrations in *Privilege* is worked out in a similar manner, only this time with even more conscious visual allusions. The opening of the film and the National Stadium sequences were not simply inspired by *Triumph of the Will*, but, because of Watkins' camera angles and *mise en scène*, they become a humorous pastiche of Leni Riefenstahl's classic propaganda film. The filming of a ticker-tape parade for Steven Shorter with the tracking shots of the crowds during the motorcade, the low angle medium shots of Shorter standing in the front of the lead car, and the close-up shots of the back of his upraised hand as he passes a throng of onlookers parallel almost exactly the footage of Hitler's ride into Nuremberg. In the stadium sequences, a rock version of "Jerusalem" replaces the "Horst Wessel Lied"; crucifixes and Steven Shorter's symbol of the arrow (designed to resemble a cross) supplant the swastikas, and the Reverend Jeremy Tate and the bishop of Essex serve as surrogate figures for Rudolf Hess and Joseph Goebbels when they review the regimented

Steven Shorter (Paul Jones) at the massive Christian Crusade rally.

Steven is about to be led off the stage after completing his song "Free Me."

masses amid an array of flags, banners, marching bands, torches, and burning crosses.

These filmic allusions and the exaggerated depiction of the director of television commercials who claims to have been influenced by the Moscow Art Theatre and of Freddie K., "musical director to Steven Shorter and self-confessed anarchist," contribute much to the satirical thrust of the film. *Privilege*, however, is not merely a broadly played satire in the Juvenalian mode. Pitted against the satiric sequences are seemingly incongruous moments, such as Butler's comments to Steven about leading the masses for a good purpose and Steven's behavior at Butler's lobster supper, which appear to be working on a different level altogether. As a result, a disquieting, ambivalent tone pervades the film, but perhaps this dichotomy of attitudes was intentional. In an unpublished retort to the British critics of *Privilege*, dated July 17, 1967, Watkins acknowledges the strange mixture of forms in the film: "*Privilege* is not a comedy, or a satire, or a realistic or an unrealistic film, or a social document, or a documentary, or a feature—it is all these things and many more, welded into a nightmare which, I believe, despite the many personal things in it, has direct relevance to everyone today."

Although the dominant narrative flow of Steven Shorter's realization of how he is manipulated in order to control the public appears essentially in chronological order, *Privilege*, as previously mentioned, is not a conventional narrative film. Watkins frequently cuts into this simple line of development with information from the narrator, photomontages, and interviews which "float" outside any pattern of chronology. The tenseness which results from these techniques reflects, according to Watkins, his own psychic tension and nervousness about the subject matter being depicted in the film. These "floating" sections account for the somewhat amorphous structure of *Privilege*, but other aspects in the film's organization also create points of tension.

First of all, in the context of a metaphorical and often wildly satirical frame, Watkins employs a voyeuristic, *cinéma vérité* camera style to record the behavior of Steven Shorter. He also attempts to create a dialectic between Shorter's almost inarticulate forages into verbal expression and his pauses and extended silences. These silences, in turn, contrast with the endless verbal onslaughts of Alvin Kirsch, Freddie K., and others in Steve's entourage. Their verbal facility, however, results in nothing more than the spewing forth of cant and promotional hype. Aside from Vanessa Ritchie, no one in Steve's plastic universe is capable of genuine communication—even on the simple level of eye contact. Alvin Kirsch is so totally narcissistic, for example, that his eye contact is reserved only for the camera or for himself in mirror reflections. Finally, Watkins' film presents a society devoid of privacy, and thus he punctuates his film with the endless popping of flashbulbs to establish an annoying flicker effect which practically forces the audience to experience viscerally the constant intrusions into Shorter's life.

Watkins does employ Shorter as a metaphor for the way in which mass media use forms of entertainment to lull and divert the public from problematic issues, but he also claims that his protagonist represents "many young people who are exploited and who do feel their individual identities entirely repressed by a self-seeking and rather ruthless system which has no truck with individuality at all." This concept is visually reinforced throughout the film by the emphasis on Shorter's handcuffs which serve as a symbol of his imprisonment. During his stage act, the police tantalizingly release Shorter from his cell and take off his cuffs. Later, the cuffs are permanently removed for the Christian Crusade rally at the National Stadium, but this release is only an illusion of freedom used to the advantage of the establishment forces. According to Watkins, "the film is indicating that when you are allowed freedom . . . it will only be when the system is sure that it can use that freedom—that the freedom is controlled and is not going to upset things in any way. Then, of course, it can use the appearance of freedom very much to counter any opposition to the centralized ethic by saying 'Ah ha, but you see what you are saying is not correct because you are free' . . . and that is a very important thing that *Privilege* is dealing with, and it has been almost entirely overlooked in critiques of the film."[6]

Privilege then is a continuation of Watkins' filmic assault on political, educational, and media structures which destroy the dignity of the individual, the growth of his imagination, and the freedom of his actions. In *Privilege*, we do not find the results of a repressive clan system or the subjection of Hungarian freedom fighters by Soviet tanks. Instead of guns, we find a less painful, more insidious method of restraint. We encounter a persuasive form of fascism concealed by the rhetoric of benevolent concern and responsibility. In a mellow yet serious voice, Andrew Goddard Butler, a bank director and chairman of Steven Shorter Enterprises Limited, explains to Steven that the masses must be controlled.

> The liberal idea that given enough education these millions will grow into self-aware creative human beings is nothing but an exploded myth. It can never happen. They're stunted little creatures with primitive emotions which are, in themselves, dangerous. They've got to be harnessed, guided; we've seen it happen over and over again for an evil purpose. Germany, Russia, China. But now we've got a chance to make it work for their own good. You, you're our chance, Steven. They identify with you. They love you. Steven, you can lead them into a better way of life. A fruitful conformity.

This is the attitude that Watkins fights against, not only in *Privilege*, but in all his work. Unfortunately, the impact of his message is somewhat muted in *Privilege* because of serious problems which, ironically enough, derive from the very aspect which attracted him to the project and inspired him to push beyond the limitations of Speight's original story—the film's self-referential dimension.

It should be clearly understood from the beginning of this discussion that Watkins is not Steven Shorter. Shorter lacks Watkins' strength, passion, anger, and commitment; he has been groomed and molded by managers, press agents, and the very values that he has come to represent. As such, the extent of his revolt is limited to an almost inarticulate, emotional cry. "I'm someone—I'm a person. (Pause.) I'm a person. I'm a person. I'm a person. I am nothing. This is me. (Pause.) Nothing. And this is you (pause) because you've made me nothing. I hate you; I hate you; I hate you." In a sense, Shorter is Watkins' version of Albert Camus' rebel. He has come to recognize that certain worthwhile things within him must be taken into account. He finally insists that his individuality is worthwhile, and this action isn't merely egotistical. As Camus has written of this rebel, "He acts, therefore, in the name of certain values which are still indeterminate but which he feels are common to himself and to all men."[7] Shorter's demand of respect for himself, then, is a demand of respect for all human beings.

It is not Shorter per se with whom Watkins identifies, but rather his predicament. Nowhere is this better illustrated than at the end of the film, when after having tried for the first time to speak honestly to the public, Steven Shorter is barred from "this and any further appearance on television, just to insure that he does not again misuse his position of privilege to disturb the public peace of mind." Clearly, this is Watkins' metaphorical depiction of his own experiences at the hands of the BBC as a result of having made *The War Game*. There are, however, two crucial differences. In all probability, Shorter is about to make an apology for his previous statements, and he is banned from television with public endorsement. Watkins never retreated from his position on *The War Game*, and many members of the British public rallied behind him when the BBC banned the film.

A "blurry edge," however, exists between Steven Shorter's *angst* and the filmmaker's, and Watkins now admits that Shorter's lashing out at those assembled for the Federated Records award banquet was a reflection of his own feelings at the time about people in media:

When in the end I had Steven Shorter stand up and face that ballroom of tuxedoed people and make that speech attacking them, that was very personal to me. I've thought about this recently, and those tuxedoed people are really my colleagues in media. . . . In a sense, I was very much hurting from that [their reaction to *The War Game*]. I think I felt myself, my own individual values, being very much attacked and suppressed by my own profession. It is that kind of hurt that much in this speech stems from. I was probably dealing with my own position very much. Of course, it is not completely logical – what I am saying, because in some ways, you could say that Shorter is attacking the public at large for making him nothing, but you must understand that in some ways I felt that about the media. I felt the media had used me when it was something successful [*Culloden*], but then it treated me like a naughty little child when it didn't want to face the consequences of what I was doing.

In using a figurative depiction of his own experience as a microcosm for suppression within media, Watkins also inad-

Watkins acts out a scene for Paul Jones during the shooting of *Privilege*.

Jones in a rehearsal of the same scene.

vertently created a situation, at the end of his film, which in a
perverse fashion could be interpreted as proof for Butler's
analysis of the public. While Watkins reflects an Orwellian
sensibility, *Privilege* is not *1984*. In the Orwell novel (which is
also self-reflexive in many ways), the suppression of the individual has reached the ultimate stage. There is no hope for
Winston Smith. In *Privilege*, the future is really a metaphor for
the present, and while "Britain in the near future" is clearly
well on its way to the world of 1984, the public in this film
should not be equated with the "proles" of Orwell's novel.
Thus, even within the metaphorical frame of Watkins' film, it
becomes extremely difficult to accept the idea that the public
would turn against Steven Shorter so suddenly and so completely.

Despite this flaw, *Privilege* remains one of Watkins' favorite
films, and the only one that he would change if he had the
opportunity.

I agree with the point that the film has a rather negative implication vis-à-vis the public at the end . . . because the public wants Steven Shorter just to go on duping them, and the moment he starts to
speak the truth out, it allows the British establishment and the Steven
Shorter management to drop him out of sight, rather than acknowl-
edging that the kind of things that he is dealing with are honest feelings and supporting him. . . . There is absolutely no doubt that inad-
vertently—and I think that it is alone of my films in falling into this
trap, at least I hope it's alone of my films—it does have a certain dismissal of the public which I very much regret now. I think if I were
ever to make that film again, the only thing that I would change
would be the last few minutes. . . . Perhaps I might do two things
with the film. First of all, I might not have Steven Shorter directly
attack the public for using him. I might have him more attacking the
management for using him and in that sense for using the public as
well—and that the public allow themselves to be used. I might have
changed it in that way, and also at the end I would have had some of
the public agreeing with Shorter. Some would turn against him (of
that there is no doubt), but some would support him, and some would
be very undecided. . . . I really can't answer for you why I didn't see
the film with that kind of broader vision. I suppose it just has to do
with this growing process. . . . I just hadn't thought my way through
all of these things yet.

Privilege is an ambitious, experimental work in which Watkins mixed together various forms and modes of filmic expression, but he failed finally to fuse them into a coherent artistic unity. To paraphrase a line from W. B. Yeats, the film's center cannot hold. The metaphorical dimensions of the film do not always follow a consistent line of development, in that Steven Shorter seems to represent too many different things at various times throughout the film. The *cinéma vérité* technique of following Shorter's activities works well in providing a voyeuristic ambience. For instance, the intruding zoom past the half-closed dressing room door after the conclusion of the stage act and the persistent tracking shot of Steven and Vanessa after Butler's lobster dinner are superb examples of form reflecting theme. Most of the interview sequences, on the other hand, lack a clearly recognizable point of reference. True, Watkins wanted tension within the film, and thus he consciously conceived "floating" sections to disrupt the narrative flow, but *Privilege* lacks that unique blending of involvement and detachment which accounted for the strong emotional and intellectual responses generated by his previous films.

Although Watkins developed his characters in *Privilege* much more than any figure in *Culloden* or *The War Game*, they still never push beyond the "representatives of people in various circumstances" level of his previous works. Indeed, one is often more concerned and involved with the Scottish Highlanders or the doctor in *The War Game* than with Steven Shorter. Even though the audience comes to see both the public and private selves of Shorter, his weakness and passivity make him somewhat unsympathetic, even in the context of the manipulation which victimizes him.

In the final analysis, *Privilege* is a mixed bag. Although not successful on a number of levels, it clearly indicated that Watkins was not going to rest on his laurels. He would experiment further not simply with techniques of reconstruction, but with a form which attempted to fuse realism with allegory and metaphor.

Gladiatorerna (*The Gladiators*)

In early 1967, after finishing *Privilege*, Watkins proposed to Universal that he make a Western dealing with the plight of the Indians. Universal Studios responded enthusiastically, and Watkins went to Hollywood to meet with Marlon Brando, who agreed to star in the film as a cavalry scout. Perhaps because Brando and other professional actors were involved in the project, Watkins conceived his script in a rather traditional manner. Dissatisfied with the finished script about a fictional Indian tribe led by Chief Iron Dog, Watkins discarded it and began work on a more factual script which he finally completed in February, 1968. The title, *Proper in the Circumstances*, was derived from an 1875 memo in which the Secretary of the Interior turned over the Indian situation to the War Department "for action as the Secretary of War may deem proper in the circumstances." This ponderous script, conceived in the documentary style of *Culloden*, covered the battles of the Washita, Powder River, the Rosebud, Little Big Horn, and Slim Buttes, but Watkins did not simply replace Scottish Highlanders and English troops with the Sioux and the United States cavalry. Counterpointing still remained the major structural device, but in this new script, characterization was more fully developed; for instance, the career of George Armstrong Custer was paralleled with the actions of Crazy Horse and Sitting Bull.

Like *Privilege*, this projected film was considerably ahead of its time. The graphic violence of the film might easily have rivaled *The Wild Bunch* (1969); the presentation of authentic Indian rituals was more accurate and less sensational than the examples seen in *A Man Called Horse* (1970), and the depiction of Indian massacres more effectively conceived than those in *Little Big Man* (1971) and *Soldier Blue* (1972). Indeed, on the basis of the shooting script, this film, had it been completed, would certainly have been one of Watkins' most powerful works and perhaps the strongest film ever made on the topic of injustices to the Indians. But *Proper in the Circumstances*, the culmination of a year's travel, research, and writing, was rejected by Universal in forty-eight hours on the grounds that the American moviegoing public would not really be interested in yet another movie about Custer and the Indians, since it already knows all there is to know about Custer.[8]

John Heyman, who would have served as executive producer for the Indian film, then encouraged Watkins to write a script for what was to become *The Gladiators*. With the assistance of Nicholas Gosling, Watkins wrote a script depicting a time in the near future when wars between nations have been replaced by lethal games that pit selected ten-man teams against each other in computer-controlled combat. The purpose of these "peace games," however, is not to promote peace, but to channel aggressive drives and to increase feelings of national pride in the millions of television viewers addicted to watching these weekly games. In this script, Watkins again returned to issues that concerned him in *Privilege* – issues such as the growing misuse of media and the siphoning off of resistance so that young people will eventually come to see the world in the so-called "proper perspective."

The actual plot of the film revolves around the playing of the 256th peace game. This game, like all the others, is being telecast live by Boglobini Spaghetti Co., which each week buys two hours of prime time on the global network in order to sponsor the world's most popular television show. The opponents in game number 256 are the Allies team (made up of members from Britain, United States, West Germany, and South Vietnam) and a Chinese team. Also attached to the allied team is B3, a rebellious French student who seeks, on his own, to find the control room and to destroy the computer ICARUS (Ideological Correction And Rapid Unification System) which controls the games. During the opening section of the game, the morale and effectiveness of the allied team rapidly deteriorate, but after a series of costly setbacks, the team captures C2, a female member of the Chinese team. B4, a member of the allied team, befriends the prisoner, and both attempt to break out of the game during a moment of chaos in which the computer's power fails. The officers watching the game immediately decide that the two traitors must be hunted down and killed, and that their deaths must be televised to the world-wide audience. Meanwhile, in his attempt to find the way to the control room, B3 restores ICARUS's power and activates the process whereby B4 and C2 are killed. B3 finally reaches the control room only to find out that, like all the others involved in the game, he has been used by the system that he is so bent on destroying.

After a shooting script was completed, Heyman withdrew from the project, but Sandrews Productions of Stockholm im-

mediately stepped in and offered to produce the film if Watkins would change the setting from England to Sweden. So in
mid-1968, prompted by personal motives and by the growing
belief that he could no longer make films in England, Watkins
moved his wife and children to Sweden.

Gosling and Watkins did not simply change the setting from
Alexander Palace in North London to a castle and an abandoned brick factory outside of Stockholm; they adjusted the
situation, the characters, and the dominant patterns of imagery
as well. Many of the changes in the script, including the expansion of the role of the Swedish colonel who serves as host
to the officers, the use of red and green lights to control the
movements of those participating in the games, and the comfortable, regulated environment in which dissenters are allowed to protest in an orderly, totally ineffectual manner, derived from Watkins' perception of Swedish society during his
initial sojourn in Stockholm. The changes in the script, however, were not made by Watkins alone. Gosling, who also came
to Sweden to work on revisions, suggests that close collaboration marked all stages of the writing of the script.

> We spent a lot of time on the script. We worked, first of all, in the
> production office in London . . . and then Peter and I went to Spain
> with his family for a couple of weeks' holiday and worked on it there
> and came back to London and finished it. . . . Later, when the script
> was sold to Sandrews, we went to Sweden and spent about three or
> four months revising the script. . . . Peter had worked out the basic
> story line, but we worked on the plot structure on our own and then
> came back and compared notes. Peter would pick which version or
> combined version that he preferred. And when it came down to
> dialogue writing, we often did that together.[9]

The revised shooting script of *The Gladiators* grew to a
cumbersome size (perhaps twice as long as the final film), and
like *Privilege*, it mingled humor, seriousness, horror, and satire. For instance, Major David S. Doubting, the host of the
television show presenting the games, was an even greater
target for satirical attack in the shooting script. Also, part of the
plot structure depended on Charles Auguste Bidet, an officer
in the French security police, and on an almost-Shakespeare-
an character in Swedish guise, a boilerman named Rundelius.
In the shooting script, Rundelius switches off the computer's
power as part of his protest against low wages and a shortened

lunch hour. Fortunately, in the final film version, Bidet was dropped altogether; Rundelius was reduced to a figure of no consequence, and a more plausible explanation for the power failure, a short circuit, was supplied. In the film itself, changes were also made in the roles of B4 and B5, who, in the shooting script, rebel against the game, leave their comrades, and attempt to reach the control room on their own. One suspects that after the 1968 May revolution in Paris, Watkins decided to combine these figures into one and to depict his left-wing radical as B3, a dissident French student.

Other differences between the shooting script and the final film version are worth noting. Although trimmed, most of the dialogue spoken by the officers in the script is found almost verbatim in the film. There was no improvisation here, and two of the central figures, the British general and the British staff officer, were portrayed by Arthur Pentelow and Frederick Danner, professional actors who also appeared in *Privilege*. In contrast to this method of presentation, however, almost all of the dialogue spoken by the combatants in the film was improvised by the nonprofessional actors who portrayed them, after engaging with Watkins in lengthy discussions about their characters. This improvisation, in turn, and the method of filming the action sequences were probably responsible for much of the soldiers' realistic responses. Watkins was especially wise to employ wide-scale improvisation in these verbal exchanges. The speeches originally attributed to the black American soldier were especially flawed in their rhythmic patterns and idiomatic usage, and in general, the dialogue among members of the B team was the weakest aspect of the shooting script.

The structure of the shooting script, as one might expect, depended on the juxtaposition of the officers watching the action on a television monitor with the combatants who fight each other with real weapons. The script, however, was unexpectedly traditional in terms of narrative flow, chronological development, and the minimal role of the narrator, who is reduced to a few lines of commentary about the origin of the peace games and to simple character identification. All of these aspects, however, were radically altered in the post-production stages of the film. Watkins has always allowed for improvisation, chance, and intuition to alter his conceptions.

With *The Gladiators*, he went one step further; he permitted much of the film's final structure, aside from a basic shape provided by the counterpointing in the script, to be discovered in the process of editing.

Although it was shot in 35mm, *The Gladiators*, like all of Watkins' films, had a high shooting ratio, and at this point in time, it is difficult to determine exactly how much of the shooting script was actually filmed and then discarded on the editing table. Among this eliminated footage was the film's most elaborate and possibly most expensive sequence—the death of B6. For this series of shots, Derek Ware was brought over from England to fall from a high tower onto an area cushioned by cardboard cartons and mattresses. Also rejected were expository sequences from the early section of the script. The removal of these sequences probably assisted in establishing the film's tenseness and pervasive visual rhythms, but it also created a difficult situation for the viewer in that the complicated rules for the peace game become unnecessarily obscure.

The fact that *The Gladiators* was shot in 35 mm also significantly affected Watkins' conception of the film while it was in production. Aware of the problems that might develop from using this film gauge, he attempted to maintain some kind of continuity in his 35mm work by hiring key technicians who assisted him on *Privilege*. Thus William Brodie became the film's art director, and Peter Suschitzky again served as director of photography. The problems with the shooting of *The Gladiators*, however, were considerably more challenging than anything encountered on *Privilege*. Suschitzky had little difficulty in achieving the nontheatrical lighting effects that Watkins desired, but there were numerous other obstacles caused by the fickle Swedish weather and by the cramped space in the passages of the abandoned factory which served as the location for the battle sequences. According to Suschitzky, Watkins quickly realized and accepted the limitations of camera movement in all the scenes dealing with the officers and, as a result, worked closely with the actors to get subtle variations of facial expression within the static framing of these figures. On the other hand, Suschitzky cannot remember being given any specific instructions about framing or camera movement for scenes dealing with the soldiers participating in

Watkins adjusts the angle of an officer's cap.

The officers study the game via closed-circuit television.

the games. It was, of course, generally understood that Suschitzky would strive for a newsreel effect to the extent that the bulky equipment and cramped space would allow.[10]

According to Watkins himself, the use of 35mm greatly affected the film's structure and

dictated the more static style of the film. I had to make very quick decisions about how to handle the fact that working with 35mm was slowing me down enormously. . . . I decided to settle for the more front-on, static style of the film at least for the officer scenes. Obviously the other scenes were more mobile, but *The Gladiators* is the most static of my films. I tried to turn a disadvantage to an advantage and incorporate a kind of static frame to be a contrast to the more rigorous newsreel style of the soldier scenes. Some of these soldier scenes are all right, but they were very, very difficult to shoot with a 35mm synchronous camera.[11]

The counterpointing between the soldiers and officers progressed beyond a mere editing device, and because of the shifting visual styles necessitated by the contingencies of the filming, Watkins evolved a type of "block structure" somewhat similar to what he employed in *The War Game*. In *The War Game*, he juxtaposed what he considered to be the "fantasy" of dominant present-day opinions about the aftermath of a nuclear explosion with the "reality" of the probable future. In *The Gladiators*, the officers devise plans of attack and defensive strategies, observe the results via television monitors, and comment on the effectiveness of the computer, but their fantasies of themselves as grand master chess players bring about the deaths of the "pawns," "knights," and "rooks" whom they maneuver through an artificial, but all-too-real battlefield.

Although the combatants in the game are in no way three-dimensional characters, their credibility as individuals stands in marked contrast to the intentionally artificial presentation of the officers. Watkins strongly objects to any description of these officers as caricatures; but that is what they are, and this term should not be interpreted by him or by the reader in a strictly pejorative sense. Caricature usually exaggerates and distorts personal qualities; but, needless to say, this kind of ridicule can have a serious political and / or social purpose and can be extremely effective in a satirical context. In *The Gladiators*, Watkins sought out representative facial types,

used exaggerated speech and behavioral patterns, and presented stereotyped political and philosophical positions to
depict the officers as archetypes for the countries they represent. As such, we encounter the ridiculously pompous British
general, the no-nonsense, efficient Chinese colonel, the
thoughtful Indian who praises idealism but ultimately accepts
pragmatism, the militarist Nigerian, and the complacent, self-
satisfied Swede. One may quarrel with a particular depiction
of national characteristics, but to do so at length is to risk missing the major argument of the film. What Watkins' film shows
is that all governments (left, right, or middle of the road) work
together to perpetuate a climate of world hate, distrust, and
aggressive antagonism in order to maintain their own nationalistic systems and value structures.

What is of minimal importance to each officer and to the
government which he represents is the fate of individuals, and
Watkins reinforces this theme visually through myriad patterns of imagery associated with lifeless objects, such as flags,
uniforms, insignias, weapons, television cameras, and the
lights of the computer panels. This attitude, however, is not
confined to the officers. B1 and some of the other soldiers become obsessed with the game to the point that the goal of
reaching the control room far outweighs the loss of human life.
Such a view is also paradoxically embraced by B3, the French
student, who wants to destroy the system for the good of humanity, but justifies violence and even kills a naive Swedish
policeman who blocks his path to the control room.

Counterpointing and recurring patterns of imagery are the
most conventional aspects of this film's structure. Of more
interest, perhaps, are brief, deliberate, seemingly minor disrup-
tions of the narrative flow and the role of the narrator.
Throughout the film, Watkins cross-cuts from the officers
watching the game on monitors, to the participants (almost exclusively the allied team), and to Captain Davidsson in the
computer control room. Continuity is maintained in part
through subtitles imposed throughout the film. These subtitles frequently indicate the progress of time in the two-hour
game. There are no flashbacks, and thus the few examples of
brief shots being repeated from earlier sections of the film,
such as a quick shot of B7 saying that he is twenty-one years of
age, seem to serve no immediately obvious function. For some

The B team under attack.

The radical French student who wants to reach the control room.

critics, the inclusion of such material was either an example of triteness or an indication of the filmmaker's lack of craftsmanship. Such, however, was not the case. Watkins' experiments with film form were not random exercises conceived as ends in themselves. His attempts to fuse expressionism with realism and documentary techniques with an allegorical framework became part of his growing conscious effort to subvert traditional documentary form and everything that this kind of filmmaking represents. When the viewer sees the repeated short shot of a seemingly minor moment in *The Gladiators*, he is forced to pause momentarily, and perhaps as a result of his slight hesitation, he might begin to consider the nature of the perspective that the film presents. From whose perspective is the viewer seeing the events depicted on the screen? The problem with *The Gladiators*, however, is that Watkins is still grappling with a form that he has not yet quite mastered, and thus the repeated shots are too few, too brief, and too cryptic to be effective in stimulating the desired thought process in most viewers.

What Watkins attempts in this film and in most of his work is to create a situation in which he involves the audience in what it is seeing through the use of realistic newsreel techniques. Part of his genius rests in his unique ability to make filmic reconstructions appear so lifelike that sections of his films seem as if they have actually happened. There were no cameras in 1746; there are no peace games, and no nuclear bomb has ever been dropped on England, but Watkins strives to present the event he is filming as if it were actually occurring. The audience knows that what it is watching could not be real, but at times, some viewers almost begin to accept for literal truth what they are seeing on the screen. At this point, Watkins often shifts techniques and perspectives to show how unlike the so-called real world this filmic representation can be. He reminds his viewers that he is a filmmaker and that they are watching his subjective film, and hopes this realization will start a process of thinking in the audience about the nature of all television programs and films in general and the so-called objectivity of documentaries and television news broadcasting in particular.

In *The Gladiators*, Watkins also tries to extend this "backthinking" process through the use of his narrator. The narrator in the final film version not only provides necessary background information, but insights about the nature of the computer, statistics about defense budgets and the changing cost of killing men in wars, and guidance to the viewer concerning the filmmaker's political position. At first, the viewer might think that the narrator is simply being used to further the illusion of a live television coverage of the games, but it soon becomes clear that this disembodied voice possesses an omniscient perspective impossible for any television commentator. While his speaking role is small, his subjective position is quite clear, and he reinforces in verbal terms the message that Watkins articulates visually.

In his conception of epic theater, Bertolt Brecht dismissed the implication and involvement of the audience in the events taking place on the stage. Instead, he wanted to turn the audience into observers who are brought to a point of recognition about the nature of the world and who then become ready to take action upon this knowledge. Watkins, however, as Raymond Durgnat wisely noted in remarks about *Privilege*, manages to have the best of both worlds. His "alienation" or detachment effects are "in the very best sense better perhaps than Brecht's, in that the lucidity co-exists with, and does not need to destroy, the spectator's emotional participation."[12] Nowhere in *The Gladiators* is this concept better illustrated than in the depiction of the deaths of B4 and C2.

Watkins brings together much of the film's imagery of objects (flags, emblems, and uniforms) in a manner to counterpoint the black and white photomontage of the beating to death of these two individuals who try to break out of the system. Cross-cut with the photomontage is live-action color footage of the British staff officer taking photographs of the group of officers. The music track from the first movement of Mahler's magnificent Third Symphony is heard throughout the sequence, and as the staff officer looks out at the camera filming him just before he clicks his own camera, a voice-over track repeats the logic for eliminating B4 and C2: "Remember, sir, two people equal one valve. Four people equal two valves. If it goes on like this, we shan't have any machine left, will we?" The final shots of the sequence juxtapose close-ups of the officers' caps with a section of the photomontage which details the hands of B4 and C2 reaching toward each other.

Clearly, the photomontage distances the viewer in one sense, and the alienation effect is increased through the music and voice of the narrator. In a paradoxical way, however, the black and white images set off these deaths as something special and, as such, involve us even more in this tragedy.

The Gladiators continues the experiments Watkins initiated in *Privilege*, but still the mingling of styles is not entirely successful in that the literal level of the film is so confusing that it detracts from the more significant metaphorical levels. Certainly, the narrator makes it clear in the beginning of the film why the games were formed: "We the peoples of the United Nations . . . have resolved to establish an International Commission from all races and creeds and political beliefs and to use this machinery for the playing of a series of military games, to be based upon the gladiatorial games of ancient Rome, and to be called *Peace Games*, to be played in special centres to be established in the non-aligned countries of the world by which purpose it is hoped to divert the aggressions of mankind towards the true fundamentals of honourable sportsmanship, and the spirit of the team." No detailed explanation, however, is ever really given for the game's scoring system. The viewer only comes to know through the course of the film that points are subtracted for delays, awarded for behavior in the face of death and for capturing enemy forces. What, however, is the specific purpose of the Chinese force beyond preventing the allied team from reaching the control room? How are they awarded points? Also on the literal level, the selection procedure for the B team must be seriously questioned. Would, for instance, any team have selected B3, the radical French student? As in *Privilege*, though, it becomes disastrous to try to work the film out exclusively in literal terms. Still, the game itself functions on a literal level, and Watkins should have taken more care in its particulars.

When one pushes beyond this basic level, the metaphorical depiction of the all-encompassing power of systematized political and social structures is superbly crafted. The peace game itself, according to Watkins, "represents the hideous game of antagonism and self-interest which a lot of the more developed world is playing today. The 'Gladiators' themselves are most of us—perhaps all of us. Not necessarily to be seen in a military sense, but playing the Game of today as dictated by the pressures of the 'system,' pushing us, driving us along well-organized channels, to get safely nowhere."[13] Like us, the various groups in the film perceive themselves as having freedom, but their freedom is simply an illusion. The soldiers can follow the yellow lights to leave the game if necessary, but peer pressure, appeals from the officers in charge, and the implied promise of rewards when they return to their respective homelands keep all of them "playing the game as hard as they can." The "hippie" young people who preach love instead of war and who maintain an uninhibited life style are easily absorbed by the system and used in the game itself. Even the officers have less control over the computer system than they realize. B3, the Marxist radical, is also used by ICARUS to help destroy the only two characters who threaten the system, and when he finally does reach the control room, he is persuaded to get to know the system. The implication, of course, is quite clear; in order to set up his own system, he must first learn how to use the machine, and once he does that, he will lose all desire to destroy it. Of all the characters in the film, only Davidsson, the computer controller, knows all along that he is being used by ICARUS. Davidsson accepts this condition because he also knows that one system merely replaces another system. As he tells B3, "Your system or someone else's—they are all the same."

The last subtitle over the last shot of the film ("13:00 P.M. 'Ready for the next Game.'") reinforces Watkins' belief that revolutionary movements can never succeed if they fight the system on its own terms. More importantly, however, the final sequence delineates the position that political and economic changes only affect the surface and never the roots of the problems afflicting our century. Reformers may find this film demoralizing and pessimistic, but then Watkins is not really a reformer in the usual sense of the word. Like the great English poet William Blake, Watkins does not want to be enslaved by another man's system. Instead of being a reformer, he is much closer to being a political visionary in his rejection of current political movements, in his insistence on denying the postulates on which systems depend, in his striving for the decentralization of all structures, and in his affirmation of the dignity and worth of individuals.

The Gladiators was given its world premiere at the Cannes

Film Festival on May 20, 1969, and opened in Stockholm in late June. The Swedish reviews generally praised Watkins' seriousness, but most of them went on to attack the film for being confused, unconnected, and boring. Many of these reviewers attacked Watkins for being a "naive" or "politically vague thinker," and Lennart Jonsson voiced one of the most frequent attacks brought against Watkins' work by those who do not understand the nature of the relationship that he seeks to establish with his audience. "The vision of the future in *The Gladiators* seems meaningless, since Watkins doesn't say anything about how we shall escape getting there, nothing about the cause of the new state of affairs. To a great extent he leaves us sticking in the mud with his desolate future."[14] The film opened in London on February 12, 1970, under the title *The Peace Game* – in order to capitalize on the controversy over *The War Game* – but was quickly dismissed or ignored by most major critics. Finally, it opened in New York on October 21, 1971, and apart from a glowing review by Judith Crist, the film was again dismissed as yet another example of Watkins' hysterical paranoia.

Punishment Park

After finishing *The Gladiators*, Watkins moved his family to Paris for a brief period until being asked to come to the United States to make a trilogy of historical films for the Learning Corporation of America. Oddly enough, these films on the American Revolution, the Civil War, and the Indian wars, were to be coproduced by a West German television station. From June to September of 1969, Watkins lived in Maryland and researched his script for a film on the Civil War. By October, he realized that the Learning Corporation would not be especially enthusiastic about a film which demythologized the Civil War by highlighting the carnage of the struggle, the opposition to the war in the North, and grim historical ironies. Although he knew that the film would never be made, he decided to "honor his obligation" and to finish the lengthy script which he called *State of the Union*. He speaks of the experience as "one of the most traumatic episodes of my life – writing a script that I knew would never be used. I finished it by January or February of the following year. It was accepted with a kind of muffled thanks and sat upon."[15] *State of the Union*, one of Watkins' most thoroughly researched scripts, intermingled an account of Lincoln's emancipation plans with the preparation and fighting of the battle of Antietam in 1862. This script later became the basis for a ninety-minute videotaped slide presentation that Watkins put together for Videotape Network in 1971.

In the spring of 1970, Watkins was about to return to Europe, when he hit upon the idea of making *Punishment Park*, a figurative depiction in documentary style of the growing polarization of political attitudes in the United States. Watkins again set his film in the near future. The escalating war in Vietnam has not only thrust the country into serious domestic turmoil but is threatening to spill over into a war with Red China as well. In order to cope with the emergency, the Nixon administration declares an "Event of Insurrection' and invokes powers granted by Title II of the 1950 Internal Security Act (the McCarran act). Detention camps are established to handle the large number of draft evaders, demonstrators, and antiwar militants who have been apprehended because "there is reasonable ground to believe" that they "probably will engage in future, possible acts of sabotage." Trial by jury is no longer necessary for those suspected of conspiracy, so a tribunal hears the cases and passes out lengthy prison sentences to the detainees, who are presumed guilty even before the hearings begin. The tribunal is chaired by a manufacturing executive (and draft-board member) and consists of a labor union official (and draft-board member), a university professor of sociology, a senator, a journalist (and draft-board member), an officer of the American Legion (and draft-board member), and a housewife who chairs an organization called "The Silent Majority for a Unified America." The detainees brought before this tribunal are represented by a university professor of law who has had little time to confer with them.

Adjacent to the area where the hearings are conducted is Bear Mountain National Punishment Park, which consists of miles of desert and an American flag. Punishment Parks are described by the United States Senate Subcommittee on Law and Order as "a necessary training for the law officers and National Guard of the country in the control of those elements which seek the violent overthrow of the United States Government and the means of providing a punitive deterrent for said subversive elements." After sentencing, the prisoners are given a choice. They may begin serving their outrageously long prison sentences, or they may attempt to fulfill their penal obligation by spending three days in Punishment Park. During these three days, they will participate in an all-too-real game in which they must travel on foot across the desert without food or water (although they are told that water will be available at the halfway point in the course). Their goal is an American flag some fifty-three miles away. Those who participate in the game are promised that if they manage to elude their pursuers and reach the flag they will not have to serve any part of their prison sentence. If they are captured, they will immediately be transported to federal prisons to begin serving their sentences. After giving the participants a two-hour head start, an armed pursuit force, consisting of three federal marshals, a unit of the National Guard, and a tactical riot squad from a city police department, give chase in jeeps and cars.

Watkins' film cross-cuts the activities of Corrective Group 637 on the desert with the tribunal examination of the members of Group 638. Group 637 breaks down into three aggregations—the militants who respond with violence, the undecided faction who finally choose violence when they realize that the authorities have lied to them about finding water at the halfway point, and a small number of nonviolent individuals who try to make it to the flag. In this deadly game, however, the authorities change the rules so that none of the participants can "win." Four from the nonviolent faction finally do arrive at the American flag only to find it blocked by a line of policemen who refuse to allow them through and who beat them when an attempt is made to reach the flag. The film ends as Corrective Group 638 is about to take its run through Punishment Park—with, of course, as the audience now realizes, the same results.

Unlike *Privilege* and *The Gladiators*, 35mm productions which at times employed film crews of up to seventy people, *Punishment Park* was shot in 16mm with a skeleton crew of no more than eight people and just one Eclair camera. The set included a tent enclosed within a larger circus-size tent for the

Filming the confrontation between the police and the pacifist defendants who managed to reach the American flag.

The police confront the television camera crew.

interior scenes, and the California desert for the exterior sequences. The actual shooting time was a mere two and a half weeks, and the production budget for the entire project was only 66,000 dollars, with an additional 25,000 dollars set aside for the blow-up to 35mm.[16]

As in all his previous projects, Watkins began with a carefully detailed script, but as the preproduction stage of the film progressed, he discarded his script and decided to cast individuals who would speak dialogue based almost entirely on their own feelings and experiences. Thus most of the people who play the defendants actually held the political attitudes they express in the film, and even many of those who serve as guards during the tribunal sequences or who are part of the pursuit force had some experience in law enforcement agencies. Some of the members of the tribunal did not fully believe the extreme right-wing positions that they represented in the film; but these individuals did have generally conservative ideas, and Watkins asked them to move to "the right" of their views and "to feel a kinship with the slight lateral movement."[17]

Most of this nonprofessional cast had never appeared on stage or before a camera. The few exceptions were members of the tribunal who belonged to a local amateur dramatic society and were cast in the film primarily because of their facial types. Mark Keats, for instance, was selected to portray Chairman Hoeger because of his uncanny resemblance to Julius Hoffman, the judge who presided over the trial of the "Chicago Seven." While the cast consisted entirely of amateurs, the crew was composed of dedicated professionals whose expertise allowed Watkins the freedom to experiment in daring and original ways. Most notable were Michael Moore, the soundman who recorded all the dialogue on-the-spot, and camerawoman Joan Churchill, who managed to be both agile and efficient while carrying a heavy, hand-held camera.

Watkins had experimented with improvisation in sections of his previous films, but in *Punishment Park*, with the exception of a few statements authenticated from newsreel footage of demonstrations, nearly complete control of the dialogue was given over to the cast members after a rough outline of the sequences was drawn up by the director. Therefore, no two takes were ever the same in terms of position of the camera, the subject being photographed, or the dialogue spoken by the actors. In the tribunal scenes, which were all shot in three days, Churchill simply weaved in and out, circled endlessly around the actors, and tried to cover action occurring in multiple areas by panning and / or zooming and then adjusting focus. The newsreel quality of the film was further enhanced by desaturating the color and by removing the traditional hard edge of the image through the use of the newly developed Harrison diffusion filters. The situation of ad-lib improvisation caused even more difficulties for soundman Moore, who had to contend with open mikes positioned before the defendant and each of the tribunal members and only a vague idea of what was going to happen next.

Watkins' experiment with improvisation in *Punishment Park* not only broke deep-seated conventions in theatrical films relating to acting and the use of scripts, but it established an entirely new dimension in his already unique approach to filmmaking. It is not simply that *Punishment Park* is his most fluid film, or that the use of improvisation provided a deeper level of realism. With this film, Watkins evolved something like a psychodrama for the participants, for himself, and for the audience as well:

> This is a film dealing with the rage developing within us—the increasing intolerance within our society. The film does not do this by pretending that this problem does not exist—on the contrary it creates a framework within which the very participants in the film release their pent-up emotions and frustrations and fears; these that are common to us all, and which are created by the pressures of contemporary society. In this way, the film states "Yes, this problem does exist . . . this is what it looks like . . . here it is in the raw and naked state . . . in this problem there are no sides . . . only a malaise common to us all. . . ."[18]

The involvement and intensity of emotions achieved by the cast, even though the characters portrayed in the film function chiefly on a metaphorical level, resulted in part because these people recreated tensions that they actually felt. As such, the "reality" of *Punishment Park* and "external reality" occasionally merged in ways that must have convinced Watkins of the psychological truth of his film. During the filming sessions, tempers flared among those of different political persuasions both on and off the set. Also, shortly after the shooting of the film, Stan Armsted, the cast member who portrays Charles Robbins, was sentenced to three years in a federal penitentiary for assaulting a police officer and was found guilty on an additional bombing charge. On at least one occasion, Watkins himself was unable to distinguish "reality" from what was being improvised for the film.

In a scene near the end of the film, Officer Edwards and his pursuit force capture most of the remaining dissidents, who, in desperation, have turned to violence. The outline for the action in the sequence called for law enforcement officials to shoot two of these young people and to capture the others. One of the takes of this sequence was filmed at the end of a particularly long and frustrating day. After the sequence was shot as planned, the remaining prisoners started to throw rocks at the National Guardsmen standing nearby. Suddenly, after being hit by one of the rocks, a young guardsman dropped to his knees and, in an almost reflex response, opened fire on the rock throwers. Watkins' first thoughts, as he saw two bodies fall to the ground, were that live ammunition had somehow gotten into a gun and that a horrible accident had transpired. The camera was still running, and Watkins' response, "Oh God! Oh, God! Cut! Cut! . . . Cut the camera," was picked up by the open microphone and later incorporated into the soundtrack of the film, since his voice was used for that of the ubiquitous BBC interviewer. What occurred, of course, was not some terrible mishap with live ammunition. The tenseness and strain of the situation caused the young man portraying a guardsman to lash out after being hit by a rock. When he opened fire, two of the actors playing prisoners simply improvised their own deaths. For Watkins, this particular incident captured something of the tension and fear responsible for the Kent State killings, when National Guardsmen opened fire on antiwar demonstrators.

It is one thing to provide a framework in which actors in a film can come to understand or even to work out their own fears, frustrations, and hate, or, as Watkins phrases it, "bring out this abscess which is in us all." It is quite another thing to create a film which allows an audience to experience a similar therapeutic response—the lancing of the abscess so to speak, "to flush out hate and lack of compassion and prejudice in so many of us."[19] Yet this is what Watkins intended in the film, and while audience reactions vary from screening to screening and from country to country, there seems to be a general consensus that the film provokes extraordinary emotional and intellectual responses. The author's own experiences in screening the film to such diverse audiences as college students, deputy United States marshals, average citizens in a small upstate New York city, and law enforcement officers at the New York State Police Academy only reinforce observations about other screenings described by James M. Welsh and Steven Philip Kramer in an interview with Watkins called "Peter Watkins: Therapeutic Cinema and the Repressive Mind" and by Scott MacDonald in "Audience Reaction to *Punishment Park*."[20] Few people have "wishy-washy" or noncommittal reactions after seeing the film; instead, their responses push toward the extremes. As a result, what commonly emerges in most discussions after the film is the very same pattern of polarization depicted in the film, only now metamorphosed to a less violent and slightly less obvious manner.

Hostility to *Punishment Park* immediately surfaces in most audiences because of its form and because it is misconstrued as an indictment against America. One especially extreme reaction after a screening even linked the film to the Communists: "It's got the Communist philosophy. Go out there and shake the people up. . . . If there are prints of it around, then the Russians have got a copy of it." Much more common, however, is the approach which assaults the director for being an Englishman and daring to make a film about American political problems at a time of crisis. Various claims are then made that Watkins is uninformed and unfair, and the film's depiction of political and social repression is conveniently dismissed as simplistic, untrue, and dangerously manipulative.

In "An Open Letter to the Press," dated January, 1972, Watkins made it quite clear that the film was not an attack on America per se and that it was not even specifically directed toward American audiences. For him, the film is a personal statement about the psychic condition of our contemporary society. The situation of polarization and confrontation presented in the film is universal, and, as such, Watkins merely communicates his vision metaphorically through a "vehicle" which depicts repression in the United States at a particular moment in time. Therefore, even though the Vietnamese War has now ended and President Nixon sits in disgrace in his San

Clemente palace, the film is neither hopelessly dated nor thematically limited. As Watkins said in 1972, "*Punishment Park* takes place tomorrow, yesterday, or five years from now."

The reasons why *Punishment Park* generates such intense reactions in audiences cannot be easily summarized; rather they must be analyzed in depth, for they reveal why, next to *Edvard Munch*, *Punishment Park* stands as Watkins' greatest cinematic achievement.

In his 1972 open letter to the press, Watkins clearly recognizes the leap that *Punishment Park* makes: "I believe that *Punishment Park* breaks new ground in my work. It is a fusion of these two seemingly contrasting elements: realism and expressionism." The phrasing here is especially significant. Watkins himself sees his film as *fusing* styles. Unlike *Privilege* and *The Gladiators*, in *Punishment Park* it is impossible to break down these contrasting styles, which essentially only served as counterpointing devices in his previous feature films. In this film, the styles are woven together in a cinematic tapestry which, while it gives the impression of an unconstrained, spontaneous recording of genuine events, actually reveals, through meticulous technical control, Watkins' own figurative and unabashedly subjective vision.

Watkins employs his familiar game motif in *Punishment Park*, but gone is the confusion about rules or any breakdown in the presentation of action at the basic story level. Also, while the peace game demanded an enormous willing suspension of disbelief to accept the "reality" of what was being filmed, the use of punishment parks in this film is not all that difficult to accept. After all, the United States government interred Japanese Americans during World War II for security reasons, and in the late sixties, rumors existed among many antiwar protestors that the idea of these camps was being resurrected for the removal of undesirable radicals. More to the point, however, is the way in which Watkins incorporates actual happenings between 1967 and 1970 in his film to heighten the illusion of reality. The tribunal hearings themselves are drawn in part from the trial of the "Chicago Seven," and the gagging of defendant Charles Robbins parallels Judge Hoffman's treatment of Bobby Seale during the court case. Throughout the film, references are made to Kent State by various characters, and the interview with the guardsman who killed two of the dissenters after being hit by a rock evokes some of the television interviews with National Guardsmen after the Kent State massacre.

In the context of the period during which the events in the film are supposed to occur, it is even believable that the United States authorities would allow television coverage of the tribunal sessions and the activities in a punishment park as part of a misguided attempt to rehabilitate wayward individuals who might be watching. Even the filming of police brutality without seizure of cameras is not beyond the scope of possibility. After all, during the 1968 protests at the Democratic Convention in Chicago, Mayor Daley's police clubbed young and old alike while television cameramen filmed the proceedings and demonstrators chanted, "The whole world is watching. The whole world is watching." Finally, it is worth mentioning that during the late 1960s, riot control forces practiced tactics by setting up mock maneuvers in which half of the group played at being "hippies" and protestors (in costume) and the other half attempted to control them and to restore order. The punishment park game is just a few steps away from such a practice.

After establishing a metaphorical depiction which is so close to the reality of the period, Watkins sweeps his viewers into the action of the film with a relentless intensity that even makes *Culloden* look tame by comparison. The pace of the film is frantic, as is the editing. There are no lulls, no diversions, no opportunities to pause and consider the validity of arguments. The tensions of an omnipresent confrontation are constantly reinforced through both the form and the content of the film, and these tensions are quickly transferred to the audience.

Watkins even alters his treatment of the narrator in *Punishment Park* to assist in maintaining the illusion of actuality. Unlike *Privilege* and *The Gladiators*, no voice informs the viewer that the events depicted take place in the near future. There is no omniscient narrator properly distanced by time and place to comment on the action from the safety and comfort of an armchair. Watkins himself supplies the voice of the on-the-spot BBC interviewer-commentator who attempts to be calm, cool, and objective in his presentation, but the impossibility of such a position becomes obvious as the film progresses. Although never seen directly, this commentator becomes a dynamic character in the film. His movement from an almost inhuman detachment to being an involved participant screaming at members of the pursuit force is commendable, and perhaps is even meant to mirror some of the reactions of cameramen covering the police treatment of demonstrators at the 1968 Democratic Convention in Chicago. In the final analysis, however, the response of an involved media person may simply not be enough, given the particular way that television is structured at present.

The interview style of *Punishment Park* is rooted in the situation depicted, in that television crews from England and West Germany are being allowed to document the events which take place in the tribunal sessions and on the desert. For the tribunal sequences, the action is filmed in newsreel fashion, with a cameraman using a telephoto lens and pulling focus in order to follow centers of interest. On the desert, similar techiques allow for coverage of the pursuit, but there are also on-the-spot interviews with both the law enforcement officers and dissidents. For these interviews and for many shots in the tribunal hearings, Watkins returns to the tight framing of close-ups which dominated *Culloden*. This framing often cuts off faces at the hairline, and thus there is little energy escaping upward, over the head and out of the frame. This method of framing coupled with the complete freedom of camera movement, both of which Watkins lost to some extent in his 35mm films, are utilized here with newfound force and intensity—thanks, in part, to the efforts of Joan Churchill.

In all of Watkins' films since *The Forgotten Faces*, people acknowledge the existence of the camera and talk directly to it. There are, nevertheless, subtle differences in each film in the way that Watkins uses this technique. Unfortunately, these distinctions have been ignored by most critics who simply attack his constant use of a newsreel style without even attempting to puzzle out why he uses it and how it has evolved in his work. In *Culloden*, the weather-beaten, scarred faces of Highland farmers and cotters forced to fight in Charlie's army gaze passively out at us. They stare at us directly and involve us in their plight in part because of their stoic resignation to the tragedy that is about to engulf them. In *The War Game*, people look into the camera to share with us their fears, their anxieties, their fatigue, and their suffering. They want us to feel

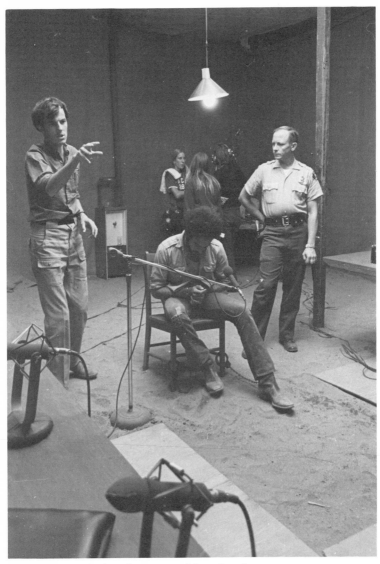

Watkins directs one of the tribunal sequences.

William Hoeger, chairman of the tribunal.

Defendant Allison Mitchner

what the aftermath of a nuclear bomb can bring. Steven Shorter and Vanessa Ritchie in *Privilege* grudgingly acknowledge the presence of the camera as part of a sustained invasion of their privacy. Most of the other characters, however, use the camera as a means of narcissistic ego fulfillment. Watkins' style is least successful in *The Gladiators* where the interviews are brief and done primarily at the beginning of the film as a means of introducing the members of "B" team. In *Punishment Park*, the interviews are often rushed and tense because of the nature of the situation depicted in the film. Also, the dissenters frequently stare out at us accusingly, with an air of defiance and anger. The police respond to the camera, of course, in an altogether different manner. For most of the film, they look into the lens with expressions of distrust, but near the end this distrust turns to hostility. Watkins' interview style can work on a number of levels from simple character introduction to character delineation, but when it is most effectively employed, it elicits some form of emotional response from an audience.

The power of the film medium rests chiefly with its emotional impact, and Watkins, like most intelligent filmmakers, clearly recognizes this fact. He frequently uses emotional involvement, however, to get his audience to come to significant intellectual conclusions. Unlike Brian de Palma and William Friedkin who seem to derive both pleasure and power from putting an audience "through the paces," as in a sophisticated Pavlovian experiment,[21] Watkins manipulates his audiences, involves them, and finally frustrates them in order to jolt them into reflecting on the nature of the medium they are experiencing. Initially, audiences rarely respond to his efforts with thanks.

In "Audience Reaction to *Punishment Park*," Scott MacDonald notes that the most frequently asked question after a screening of the film seeks to determine if punishment parks actually existed. MacDonald speculates that generally the questioner is reasonably convinced that they did not exist but needs reassurance. Once this security is provided, hostile responses rapidly multiply. Many members of the audience feel cheated or tricked because something distinctly false has been presented to them as if it were true. This response is not limited to the uninitiated or to the unsophisticated. For example, in a review of *Punishment Park* in the London *Sunday Tele-graph* of February 13, 1972, film critic Margaret Hinxman "cannot help wondering, too, about the morality of filming a fake situation (however possible or imminent) not as realistic fiction but as instant newsreel documentary." Indeed, for Hinxman, there seems to be something inviolate about documentary form, and thus no concern, no matter how geniune, can "excuse the assumption that you can picture as fact in the style of fact what is not scrupulously fact."

Documentary forms, even the newsreel, must not be viewed as sacred cows, and perhaps Hinxman should have carried her analysis a bit further. Does documentary form really allow for the objective presentation of fact? Does the mere presence of the camera alter the event? Does the cameraman merely depict his own limited perspective of the event? Does the editor shape the event? Can a newsreel contain fabrication? Can "the style of fact" deal with opinion and / or speculation? Is there really such a thing as "the style of fact"?

These are the kinds of questions about documentary raised by *Punishment Park* in particular and Peter Watkins' films in general, and as such, that is why Watkins would not have survived very long at the BBC, even if *The War Game* controversy had never occurred. The BBC's *Principles and Practice in Documentary Programmes* clearly indicates that a producer / director intent on expressing his own personal views in films, "should leave the BBC and make his name in some other field." For the BBC, the conventions of documentary form and the illusion of maintaining objectivity must be upheld in order to sustain the faith and trust that television audiences have in news and public affairs programming. This fear of losing credibility is not limited to the BBC. A number of years ago in the United States, David Wolper produced a television series which merged "fact" and "fiction" by blending excerpts from stock newsreel footage with dramatic reenactments. Executives of CBS News strongly objected to Wolper's methods, "feeling that the use of such techniques might eventually raise suspicions that all news footage could be so easily manipulated."[22]

Too many television executives and members of the public unfortunately view the evening news reports as the objective presentation of truth–the gospel according to Cronkite, or

Walters, or Brinkley. The healthy skepticism contained in the maxim, "Don't believe everything you read in the newspapers," may still apply to the print medium, but in this age of the image, we should not forget that this caution must apply to television and film as well. The manipulation that takes place on the evening news is, of course, quite different from that found in the Wolper series or in *Punishment Park*, but it is a form of manipulation nonetheless.

Punishment Park concerns itself with much more than the subversion of traditional documentary form, and its effectiveness in arousing an audience extends far beyond the presentation of a metaphorical vision in newsreel style. In fact, *Punishment Park* is not even developed in a typical linear fashion. The extensive cross-cutting creates complex interactions which often do not further the narrative line as much as they allow for multiple perspectives and ironic interplay. Within this intricate structure, Watkins inserts a few, quick repeated shots, as he did in *The Gladiators*, to further break down the nominally chronological pattern of organization. When Officer Edwards' voice is heard explaining to the participants that their stay in Punishment Park will be as violent as they make it, the game has already started, and the images which accompany his words again force us to look at the police subduing the young man who tried to escape even before the pursuit began. Also, later in the film after they have been killed, Watkins ironically repeats scenes from an interview with the two militants who claim that the authorities are playing a game with them: "You either win, or you die." More to the point, however, is the fact that *mise en scène*, visual motifs, sound, and, most significantly, editing are employed in ways totally antithetical to anything found in newsreels.

Given the circumstances in filming *Punishment Park*, it was impossible for Watkins to control very much of the composition of shots, especially for the material taken in the tribunal tent. Nonetheless, from the sizable amount of tribunal footage available to him (about 20,000 feet), he frequently chose shots which contained multiple levels of activity and information within the *mise en scène*. When defendants respond to the tribunal, they are often filmed in the middle ground of the frame, with an officer in the background and the edge of a table in the foreground. The information within the shot assists in defining the relationship of the defendant to those in charge, but the compositional pattern assumes additional meaning when viewed in relationship to other shots. The officer in the background is often seen only from the chest down, and since he stands directly behind the seated defendant, the defendant's head is flanked on one side by a holstered gun and on the other side by a billy club attached to the officer's belt. This preoccupation with symbolic objects assists in establishing a pattern of visual images much like the "object motif" found in *The Gladiators*. There are numerous close-up shots of guns, billy clubs, handcuffs and shackles on the defendants, and, of course, the American flag to emphasize the repressive goals of the authorities and their total control of "the game." Further tension from the composition of the specific shot under discussion is derived from the table in the foreground. On the table is a pitcher of water and glasses for the tribunal members who can quench their thirst at any time. Also in the *mise en scène* of some of the shots composed in this manner is a water cooler in the background of the frame. No water is offered to the defendants during the hearing or, more importantly, to those dissidents out on the punishment park course. The tension between these shots at the tribunal hearing and the desert shots increase as the film progresses and Harold, the nonviolent poet, finally dies because of a severe loss of body fluids.

If Watkins allowed almost complete freedom to the actors in improvising their responses and reasonable freedom to the technicians to capture all of the action in newsreel fashion, he exercised rigid control of the film in the use of sound and in editing.

Watkins experimented briefly with sound in some of his previous films, but nothing in any of them remotely foreshadows the intricate use of sound in *Punishment Park*. Possibly one of the reasons for the complexity of sound in this film is that Watkins actually edited much of the footage himself. He had been trained as an editor at World-wide Pictures, had cut his amateur films, and had worked closely with all the editors of his professional films. With *Punishment Park*, however, he and Terry Hodel sat at Steenbeck moviolas and worked through the 58,000 feet of film, deciding which takes to use and then running through endless combinations and permutations of shots. Even after the visual arrangement of shots in certain sequences was determined, changes were made in the soundtrack. These alterations often affected the dynamics of the sequences in such a way that the combination of shots would have to be reworked yet again in terms of both sound and image. This meticulous process resulted in sound montages as vital and complex as the visual qualities of the film.

To begin with, the improvised dialogue itself supplies a rather sizable amount of the film's tensions. During the tribunal sequences, people scream at each other in anger and frustration. There is constant interruption, with multiple voices all shouting at once. The defendants and the tribunal members never really talk *to* each other; they only yell *at* each other. As such, much of the sound-sync track reinforces the film's visual motifs which establish our contemporary world as a place in which people reduce each other to objects or animals. A member of the tribunal exemplifies this attitude when he tells the interviewer about punishing his own daughter. "You know, you've got to remember that these children of ours today are much like skilled and trained highly bred horses, you know. They're trained to go around that track, but then you've sort of got to hold them in, because if you let the reins out, why, after all, they'll just run around that track without any control at all. . . ."

Watkins also occasionally cuts off the dialogue track from the tribunal scenes but permits the images to continue, or he allows the dialogue track to run over nonsynchronous images so that the words take on additional, often ironic, meaning. In the desert, the sound of the pursuit force, the gun shots from the various confrontations with the dissidents, the interviews, and the commentary of the BBC interviewer create further tension—either in themselves or because of juxtaposition created by constant counterpoint editing. Over the basic sound-sync tracks of the film, Watkins frequently adds a sound effects track which includes gun shots, explosions, fire sirens, automatic weapons fire, rocket fire, helicopters, jets, and bullhorns. This track and a sound-over radio track provide an historical backdrop for the activities depicted in the film, and furthermore graphically indicate the violence taking place in the outside world, a violence which is mirrored in the microcosm of *Punishment Park*. The radio broadcasts not only cover the violence occurring throughout the nation and the world, but also the political and social repercussions as well. Beyond this, the radio track works with visual images to establish and augment rhythms and motifs or to provide startling juxtapositions. The weather reports increase the visual tension created by the desert sequences, and news items, like Nixon's "United States is a symbol of progress, hope, and justice" telegram greeting to an artists' variety show reception, supply a touch of Watkins' grim irony.

Aside from combining these multiple sound tracks, Watkins commissioned yet another track for the additional increase of tension. Using various percussive instruments, Paul Motian, a noted jazz drummer, created a score which Watkins distorted, often to the point of its being unidentifiable as percussive sounds. This track was then used sparingly but powerfully, often to overlay other tracks in order to grate further on the frayed nerves of the audience.

The intensity of *Punishment Park* also owes much to the visual tensions established through the editing, which took eight months of full-time work to complete. The narrative line of *Punishment Park* demanded a complex editing strategy in order to keep the film from fracturing into two parts. If Watkins had followed the activities of a single corrective group in a straight-forward chronological manner, the film would have had two climaxes: one at the end of the tribunal hearings and one at the end of the run through the Punishment Park course. Thus by cross-cutting between two separate groups, Watkins preserved structural unity and increased the intensity of the film on its fundamental story level. However, to say merely that *Punishment Park*, like all of Watkins' previous films, employs counterpoint editing is to do the film a serious disservice. Watkins' counterpoint structure, like his interview style, his use of narrator, and his experiments with color and lighting, has evolved in intricate, subtle ways over the years.

The cross-cutting in *Punishment Park* was not employed simply because of the demands of the narrative, and the film does not merely juxtapose Corrective Groups 637 and 638. The editing style also derives from Watkins' avowed intention of forcing audiences to directly confront the "various forces and tensions within our society." As such, the counterpointing of multiple ideas is always supported on a stylistic level as well: short shot montages juxtapose high angles and low angles, verticals and horizontals, long shots and close-ups, interiors and exteriors, open frame shots and closed frame shots, etc. The counterpointing even on the levels of plot and theme are especially complex. The defendants at the tribunal are contrasted with those hearing their case, with law enforcement officers both in the tent and on the Punishment Park course, with the television interviewer, and finally with the radicals who make up Group 637. There are, however, different attitudes within each group. The radicals already in Punishment Park break down into three distinct factions: the militants, the "semimilitants" (Watkins' term), and the pacifists. The militants believe that they can and must wreck the establishment through violence. Their inflexibility causes them to have utter contempt for their nonviolent colleagues and ultimately to mirror the inhumanity and intolerance of their pursuers. The semimilitants come to accept violence as necessary when they realize that the authorities have changed the rules during the game. The pacifists rightly perceive that the authorities are attempting to provoke them so that they can eliminate them, but they wrongly believe that they can change the system by playing according to the rules. Things will not "come out all right if they make it to the flag."

There are even different attitudes among the various law enforcement officials. Watson, the National Guardsman who "accidentally" opened fire on the dissidents, is terrified by his actions, but Officer Edwards enjoys his job and shows no sign of compassion or remorse after he kills a number of young people. Even on the tribunal, there are noteworthy distinctions to be made. Chairman Hoeger's hatred and unfairness are obvious throughout the film, but Paul Reynolds, the union steward, while not exactly a sympathetic figure, can at least be tolerated on a human level. His desire to protect his family's security and his fears for the future are understandable in the context of the hate and polarization depicted in the film.

Watkins has been widely criticized for his portrayal of the characters in *Punishment Park*, and admittedly they are not three-dimensional figures. Their shallowness, in part, derives from the situation in which we see them. There can be little depth in a shouting match in which both sides hurl clichéd political rhetoric at each other, or in characters trying to avoid capture while running miles across the desert. The characters here, like most of those in his previous films, are "representatives of people in various circumstances." They are not caricatures, like the officers in *The Gladiators*, and Watkins does not treat them as such. Occasionally, he may insert a devastating close-up to dissect a member of the tribunal, but there are no artificially exaggerated facial expressions or any mockery of physical characteristics. Since the characters in *Punishment Park* represent various intellectual positions, one suspects that Watkins loosely modeled some of them on actual personalities. Charles Robbins obviously parallels Bobby Seale; Lee Robert Brown and Nancy Jane Smith suggest shades LeRoi Jones and Joan Baez, and perhaps there is something of Tom Hayden in Jay Kaufman. Still, these actors improvised their own lines based on their perceptions, experiences, and opinions of recent American sociopolitical life.

Watkins may have attempted to heighten realism through the use of amateur actors, large-scale improvisation, and newsreel camera techniques, but like Sergei Eisenstein, he does not believe that the filmmaker should merely be a passive transmitter who reproduces "reality." For both men, the rigid control of certain technical areas, principally editing, reflects the filmmaker's personal vision and guarantees audience involvement. For Eisenstein, the human mind works dialectically by synthesizing opposing elements. Therefore, an effective filmmaker uses techniques to allow the audience to participate in bringing about meaning in a film. "The film's job," according to Eisenstein, "is to make the audience 'help itself,' not to 'entertain' it. To grip, not to amuse. To furnish the audience with cartridges, not to dissipate the energies that it brought into the theatre."[23] Watkins would probably agree with this definition of the role of film in today's society, but whether he would agree with the kind of "cartridges" that Eisenstein wanted to furnish to his audiences is another question altogether. Film for Eisenstein was the preeminent propaganda tool, and many of his films, although personal visions of history, were meant to serve "the revolution."

In *Punishment Park*, the BBC interviewer asks Harold, one of the pacifists on the desert, if his poetry is committed to the revolution. The young man's reply, "It's not committed to the revolution; it's committed to sanity," could also very well serve as Watkins' motto. Although in the early phase of his career he made what he now calls "strong personal propaganda films," by the time he conceived *Punishment Park*, his ideas about the nature and purpose of filmmaking had pushed far beyond the realm of propaganda. *Punishment Park* is not "a political tract" as *Newsweek* called it; the film was meant to serve as a catalyst for the viewer. It was Watkins' hope "that *Punishment Park* – in the same raw and admittedly painful manner as stage one in a psychiatric confrontation – will lead forward to a reevaluation of one's own human relationship, to seeking a new and more meaningful solution to the present human dilemma posed within Western society."[24]

As such, *Punishment Park* assaults the viewer with the clash of ideas in true dialectic form; there is no glorification of characters or their political positions, no advocating of alternatives, and no facile solutions. Even the "involved" position of the television interviewer is undercut at the end of the film by the policeman who points out that the interviewer and his crew did not halt their filming to help anyone. Watkins has written that in the problems depicted in the film "there are no sides," but this statement does not mean that he is "neutral" or "objective" in his presentation. Watkins is clearly opposed to repression, to brutalization (both psychological and physical), to the lack of compassion in our society, and to the false claims of our sociopolitical structures that they allow freedom.

Punishment Park exposes the viewer to what Watkins perceives to be a psychological statement about the condition of our society, so that, in Eisenstein's term, the audience may "help itself." Some viewers, however, resent the demands that the film makes of them and lash out at Watkins for being pessimistic and / or for not supplying solutions to the problems he depicts in his work. The filmmaker's reply to such attacks is often caustic and blunt:

I should have thought that you would have been bloody glad that I don't come out with a silver tray with answer 475 and say, "Here you are, darling; go home and take this piece of dogma." . . . If I were a pessimist, I would have made Laurel and Hardy reruns since 1965. I think our society is totally caught up in the abuse and misuse of these words "optimistic" and "pessimistic." I don't believe that one is pessimistic to look at very real problems that we are involved in. . . . I think I am an optimist to talk about these problems in the sense that if

I didn't talk about them, it would be because I couldn't care less about humanity or the potential of mankind. But I do care very much, which I think is optimistic. I care enough to make these films. I also care enough about your own sense of responsibility not to do what is done with you every day in your life—in education, in television—which is to force feed you with directives, force feed you with answers, force feed you with directions to move in—until you are zapped left, right, up and down. I won't do that to you. I will try and show you a problem as hard and as strongly as I can; but what to do about it even if I had the answer, which I don't usually, I would never give to you. I would never reveal it. I would chew it over in my own head, because I would leave you to try to develop your own strength to find the answer.[25]

Punishment Park is probably the most important political film of the 1960s and early 1970s, but unlike Haskell Wexler's *Medium Cool* (1969) and Robert Kramer's *Ice* (1969) which at least received limited distribution in large American cities, Watkins' film was withdrawn from commercial exhibition after a four-day run in New York City and a ten-day run in San Francisco. Watkins won the Best Director's Award for *Punishment Park* at the 1971 Atlanta Film Festival, but after a screening of the film at the New York Film Festival, the established East Coast critics attacked the film with particular viciousness. The one exception, Arthur Knight in *Saturday Review*, called the film "extraordinary" and later voted the film "one of the ten best of all time" in a *Sight and Sound* survey. However, immediately after the publication of reviews by Judith Crist ("Haters can have a field day with *Punishment Park*, the most offensive of the N.Y. Festival films I have seen to date") and Vincent Canby (". . . it is, essentially, the wish-fulfilling dream of a masochist"), Sherpix, Inc. withdrew from its contractual agreement to distribute the film. Watkins then personally approached a number of exhibitors and distributors who refused to show the film. Some of these told him: "You have a fine film there, but it is too hot a political potato to handle." and "I could never show that film. If I did, I would have the F.B.I., the Sheriff's Department, the local school board all down my neck." The two exhibitors who briefly played the film gave no reason other than "poor attendance" for its abrupt withdrawal.[26]

In his essay, *"Punishment Park* and Dissent in the West," Watkins discusses at length the problems involved in trying to distribute films like *Punishment Park* in the United States, but perhaps his most perceptive observations about the unfavorable critical responses to the film are found in an interview he gave to the British publication *Time Out*. Watkins argues that *Punishment Park* cannot be discussed in terms of being "art" and therefore attacked or praised primarily on an aesthetic level the way Ken Russell's films can. Watkins claims that *The Devils* may be "an important film that connects with 'now,'" but he argues that few critics saw the connection between the horrors of the society depicted in the film and our own:

> No, they will say that this [*The Devils*] is a "fantastic" or a "debauched" film . . . "to be seen" or "not to be seen." But they're dealing with it on a completely superficial level which is not taking the real emotive power of film to its Nth and logical conclusion. A film like *Punishment Park*, I think, by nature of the earthiness or the crudeness or the roughness or the directness with which it is made, circumvents that first level completely: you just can't handle it, and thus you are only forced to deal with it on the second level—which is why it's so unpopular, often.[27]

In *Punishment Park*, Watkins tried to take "the real emotive power of film to its Nth and logical conclusion," and he has suffered accordingly. Some of the same types of critical attacks brought against this film have been reiterated by critics of Watkins' recent Scandinavian works: *The 70s People, The Trap,* and *Evening Land*. The one exception, *Edvard Munch*, is perhaps Watkins' most successful experiment with the "emotive power" of film, but it has been perceived by most critics as an "art" film and praised—but often only on the most superficial level.

The death of Harold, the poet.

Watkins and Joan Churchill setting up a shot.

4

Edvard Munch: Film Biography as Self-Portrait and Exemplum

IF PETER WATKINS had made no other film besides *Edvard Munch*, his niche in film history would have been assured. The Munch film, however, is not some lucky fluke in his career; it did not spring from his head full-grown in Athena-like fashion. Just as the amateur films were vital in establishing the style of *Culloden*, all of his professional films stand behind the revolutionary innovations of *Edvard Munch*.

From his earliest days as a filmmaker, Watkins has sought to push beyond the traditions of conventional cinema. He has experimented with the fracturing of narrative structure to the point that his editing techniques have become a stylistic hallmark. In *Punishment Park*, he finally achieved aural montages equal in complexity to his visual arrangements, but nowhere in his canon are the relationships between sound and image as complicated as those found in the Munch film. Other technical advances explored in the earlier films, especially the blending of realistic and expressionistic styles and the use and control of color are furthered here in subtle, original ways. *Edvard Munch* also advances many of the reconstruction techniques that he had developed over the years. The film manages to achieve the near-impossible; it provides a unique balance between the actuality of Munch's statements and the improvisations of nonprofessional actors expressing their own feelings and concerns. This union is not an artificial one. It reflects, in part, the director's theory of history: "I believe that we are all history, past, present, future, all participating in a common sharing and sensing of experiences which flow about us, forwards and backwards, sometimes simultaneously, without limitations from time or space."[1] Thus the film functions on multiple levels—it delineates Munch's own fears and anx-

125

ieties, provides penetrating insight into the nature of his artistic creation, captures accurately the historical nuances of the era in which he lived, and finally allows the viewers to perceive, in this intricate amalgam, problems of contemporary society which touch them directly. As such *Edvard Munch* is a work of monumental magnitude, nearly epic in scope and scale. Yet almost paradoxically it is Watkins' most personal, most subjective film—a film which reflects many of his own feelings about relationships between men and women and about the conflict between the committed individual and a repressive social order which seeks to encompass him.

The idea for a film on Edvard Munch originated in the winter of 1968. While he was editing *The Gladiators* in Stockholm, Watkins was invited to Oslo to discuss *Culloden* and *The War Game* after screenings arranged by university students. By chance, one of these screenings took place in the auditorium of the Munch Museum, and it was at this time that the filmmaker first encountered Munch's work:

> . . . I walked around the main gallery, accompanied by a Norwegian film producer. I had never seen any of Edvard Munch's work before, and, as best I can recall, had never even heard of him. However, I was immediately—and very strongly—moved by what I saw, and felt. I recall that one of the first paintings I saw was *Death in the Sickroom*, and the impression of Munch's sister, Inger, staring straight out of the canvas at me, was something that I shall never forget. I then saw the other major works which were being exhibited at the time, including *Madonna* and *Vampire*.

Watkins expressed interest in making a film about Munch to the Norwegian producer with him, and this man, in turn, introduced him to Pål Hougen, the director of the Munch Museum, and to other Munch scholars. Little by little, he began to gather material on the artist's life, but from 1969 through the spring of 1971, he was in the United States involved in other projects. During this period, the Documentary Department of Norsk Rikskringkasting and the Drama Department of Sveriges Radio agreed to finance the projected film, but the NRK Documentary Department soon withdrew from the project because an important official objected to Watkins' brief outline of how he wanted to deal with Munch in the film. Fortunately, Lars Löfgren of Sveriges Radio supported the project on his own until he convinced the Drama Department of NRK to coproduce the film. In 1971, research began in earnest with the full cooperation of the Munch Museum. This allowed Watkins and a translator access to Munch's unpublished diaries, journals, and a thinly disguised autobiographical narrative, *From the City of Free Love*. Originally, the shooting was scheduled to begin in June, 1972, but Watkins asked for an extension of time in order to complete the research phase of the film. The revised shooting schedule of *Edvard Munch* allowed for the winter sequences to be shot during February and March of 1973 and the summer sequences to be filmed in May and June, but because the winter was so mild in Norway that year, Watkins had to use plastic snow to film additional snow sequences in May. After completion of the filming, Watkins sequestered himself for eight months in order to work full time on editing *Edvard Munch*. The finished film ran slightly over three and a half hours and was telecast in two parts on November 12 and 13, 1974, by both NRK and SR.

Although Watkins was not even thinking about the nature of biography films when he made *Edvard Munch*, the film promises to have a profound impact on this frequently ignored genre. When they are considered by critics, film biographies are almost universally pigeonholed into two categories: the romantic Hollywood popularization and the faithful, often plodding, factual documentary. The best of the first type is epitomized by the numerous "biopics"—*The Story of Louis Pasteur* (1935), *The Life of Emile Zola* (1937), *Juarez* (1939), *Dr. Ehrlich's Magic Bullet* (1940), etc.—directed by William Dieterle for Warner Brothers, while the worst is embodied in the superficial schmaltz of Charles Vidor, who specialized in glossy portraits of artists—*A Song to Remember* (1945), *Hans Christian Anderson* (1952), *Song Without End* (1960), etc. All of these Hollywood "biopics" falsify facts in order to heighten the dramatic impact, to soften character faults, or to allow for moments of inspirational creation in films depicting artists at work. At the other end of the spectrum is the factual presentation, perhaps best represented by Charles Frend's *Scott of the Antarctic* (1949) and those British television documentaries of the fifties and early sixties which pasted together newsreel footage, music, and commentary.

Ken Russell made *Prokofiev —Portrait of a Soviet Composer* (1961), his first film biography about an artist, while trapped within this "splicing together" format, but he constantly experimented with evolving new methods of approaching his subjects. His adventurous methods of connecting divergent elements and of describing the inner movements of his characters began in *The Debussy Film* (1965) and have continued through his most recent television films about Wordsworth and Coleridge: *William and Dorothy* (1978) and *The Rime of the Ancient Mariner* (1978). In his best films, Russell weaves together facts, speculations, and conjectures into penetrating, visually stunning glimpses of his protagonists. These complex, frequently ambivalent portraits also derive from the manipulation of a tripartite perspective which incorporates the protagonist's own romantic self-image, a more "objective" view, and finally the director's personal vision of his subject which is revealed through editing, patterns of aural / visual imagery, and the structure. In a Russell film, these three viewpoints are often played off against each other, and the importance of each aspect varies from film to film depending on Russell's attitude toward the protagonist.[2] It is this complex approach to the depiction of an individual's life that stands as Russell's most significant contribution to the art of biography film. However, in many of his most recent theatrical features (*Mahler, Lisztomania*, and *Valentino*), Russell simply uses the artist's life as a point of departure for an excursion primarily into the filmmaker's personal vision. As such, biographical facts are eclipsed by metaphorical representations.

Although neither an admirer nor an imitator of Russell's films, Watkins, in his massive film biography of the great Norwegian expressionist painter, carries on and pushes far beyond some of Russell's innovations. Most significantly, Watkins manages to fuse an intensely personal vision, an historically accurate depiction, and even a kind of microcosmic representation in such a manner that no dimension of the film ever infringes on the integrity of the others.

It is not just that *Edvard Munch* uses authentic settings and offers a reliable depiction of the external events of the painter's life. Watkins' film is unique among "biopics" in that it presents a number of hitherto unknown facts about Munch's life which the director carefully culled from the painter's unpublished diaries. This film is also the only work in any medium to deal with the impact on Munch of the woman referred to in the diaries as "Mrs. Heiberg." As such, the film presents a major challenge to what Watkins calls "the art historians' limited way of writing about an artist," only in terms of artistic influences rather than as an attempt to relate his personal life to his art.

Although all of his diaries and excursions into autobiographical fiction can be found in the archives of the Munch Museum in Oslo, few of the biographers or art historians who have written about Munch have incorporated very much of this material into their studies. When quotations are cited from the diaries, they usually turn out to be ones already cited by previous writers, such as the description of the last Christmas Munch spent with his mother or the entry about how disease, insanity, and death attended his cradle and have followed him throughout his life. Thus, since a major portion of what is spoken by Geir Westby (who portrays Munch) and much that is recounted by the narrator (Watkins himself) derive directly from the diaries, Watkins' *Edvard Munch* becomes one of very few film biographies to have importance as a nearly indispensable work for all future studies of the subject depicted.

Aside from being the primary source for the events reconstructed in the film, Munch's diaries may have influenced Watkins in determining the structure of the film, since Munch's modes of writing parallel, to some extent, the methods employed by Watkins in organizing the material presented in the film. Watkins himself describes Munch's diaries in the following manner:

Written sometimes in the "I" form, sometimes referring to himself as "he," "Karleman," "Brandt," or "Nansen," Munch let the surge of his feelings judder from his pen, feelings about his art, life, death, his family, and women. It is said that Munch spoke in spurts—certainly, this is how he writes. He often does not use the full-stop or comma—instead, he connects together threads of feeling, visual recall, longing, sadness, loathing, by a short stroke—thus, in one sentence or block of words he writes of the last Christmas with his mother in 1868—then in the next moment he is writing of his fatigue and despair twenty years later in visiting the frame-makers—then abruptly he enters the next paragraph with feelings of anger and sorrow about his father. Suddenly, Munch will again jump—to his remembrance of the first time he kissed "Mrs. Heiberg"—and even within his description of the same "event" or experience, Munch will move—without lifting the pen—from tenderness to extreme loathing."

Watkins' editing techniques in *Edvard Munch* go far beyond any attempt to duplicate the methods of the diaries, but it is noteworthy that the form of the film is especially appropriate for the portrayal of the private world of this particular artist. Film form mirrors subject matter in other areas as well. Munch's major source of inspiration was his own subjective experience. "I paint, not what I see, but what I saw." His subject was himself, but the self as epitomizing the psychic condition of modern man. His *Frieze of Life* was first called *Cycles from Modern Soul Life*. Therefore, what began as haunting memories or deep, personal feelings were translated into pictorial symbols and motifs which recurred in his work as part of an attempt to communicate the universal qualities of his experiences. Each painting was distinct, but when combined, Munch believed they would create a comprehensive statement about modern life. Each painting could be viewed separately, "but its full meaning would not be revealed except within the coordination of commentary provided by the remainder of the series."[3] Watkins' film strives to do the same thing. Effects are cumulative. Isolated shots are important, but meaning in the film is found chiefly in the repetitions and combinations of shots. Leitmotifs dance through the montage of shots, and images are frequently repeated in an attempt to illustrate how key experiences haunted Munch and how, if the experiences themselves are not universal, the emotions generated by them are.

Of the new information that Watkins has unearthed about Munch, the most important is assuredly the role of the relationship of the painter with "Mrs. Heiberg." Of all the books written about Munch, only Reinhold Heller's slim volume, *Edvard Munch: The Scream*, mentions "Mrs. Heiberg," but it does so in two pages chiefly to suggest that the artist, through his affair with this married woman, recognized jealousy as the major weakness of Hans Jaeger's doctrine of free love. Still, Heller notes that even after their affair ended, Munch still thought of "Mrs. Heiberg" and of her significance in his life. Recent Norwegian writers on Munch have been especially awkward in their treatment of this particular relationship, which obviously occupies a sizable portion of the artist's journals. Nic. Stang, husband of Ragna Stang, former director of the Munch Museum, remarks that "more than anyone else, Munch became the painter who painted his life, his innermost feelings as well as outer experiences." Although he makes reasonable use of Munch's journals in his book, *Edvard Munch*, Stang never mentions Munch's feelings about and experiences with "Mrs. Heiberg." The closest reference is the following sentence. "In a letter never posted, written to a Norwegian woman, he writes about the moonlit evening."[4]

It must be clearly understood that Watkins is no scandalmonger bent on revelling in the intimacies of an artist's love life. The depiction of Munch's relationship with "Mrs. Heiberg" is crucial to the dispelling of any stereotyped, simplistic notion that Munch was a misogynist whose paintings can be best understood by analyzing them as manifestations of his hatred and rejection of women. Even more crucial is the presentation of Munch's affair with "Mrs. Heiberg" not merely as offering some biographical interpretation of the subject matter of his paintings, but as a means of explaining aspects of his technique.

Munch (Geir Westby) and "Mrs. Heiberg" (Gro Fraas).

Aside from piecing together cryptic references from the diaries, Watkins discovered the actual identity of "Mrs. Heiberg," the exact place of her first meeting with Munch, and the time span during which they were emotionally involved with each other. The most intense period of their relationship coincides with the twelve-month span in 1885-1886 during which Munch worked on *The Sick Child*. The importance of this painting in Munch's canon cannot be overestimated. Munch himself said that "the painting opened a new road in my art. Most of my later work owes its origin to this very picture, which created more offense in Norway than any of my other work."[5] In the film, therefore, the sequences depicting the actual painting of *The Sick Child* are among the most revealing of Munch's creative process—in part because Watkins refuses to divorce the personal aspects of Munch's life from the so-called professional side. Instead, he suggests that it is not enough simply to view this massive painting as a study capturing the artist's feelings about the death of his sister, Sophia, and the narrator of the film stresses that the painting evolves the way it does, at least in part, as a result of Munch's relationship with "Mrs. Heiberg":

Seeking now to de-emphasize all unimportant details by blurring their images—struggling to eliminate Mrs. Heiberg from his mind—striving somehow to impart the quiver and intensity of his feelings onto the raw surface of his canvas—seeking to awaken a similar mood in the viewer—Munch works and reworks the head of his sister—detailing hair, eyes, and mouth—only to scrape the oil from the canvas and begin again. Using his knife, the back of his brush, the point of a pencil, Munch scratches and scores deep into the thick oil, as he struggles to remember, and struggles to forget.

Although Pål Hougen, former director of the Munch Museum, personally feels that "Mrs. Heiberg" dominated Munch's written material much more than she ever did his life, he also insists that Watkins was "completely right" in his conception of her effect on the creation of *The Sick Child*. Furthermore, Hougen argues that, aside from a few minor factual errors, the film is an accurate and "in no way misleading" interpretation of Munch.[6]

The ability of *Edvard Munch* to delineate believably the nature of the creative act and to elicit the feeling that the characters we see on the screen are actually involved in the painting process has been duly noted by almost all the critics who have reviewed the film. Part of the success in this area comes from using actual locations (including the probable room in which Munch's mother died), maintaining authenticity in the reconstruction of locations, having painters build up copies of Munch's work at various stages of completion, and accurately reproducing the methods that Munch actually used in the creation of his woodcuts and lithographs. Finally, the film audience is engulfed in visuals which constantly bring to mind Munch's paintings. The characters in the film do not simply resemble the figures found in Munch's work; the ambience and spatial composition of Watkins' shots often evoke the paintings. For instance, in one shot Munch sits in a beer hall in the left foreground of the frame, while "Mrs. Heiberg" and her husband are seen in the background. These individuals are not the models for Munch's *Jealousy*; but the arrangement of space in this and other shots is strikingly similar to that painting, and the emotion conveyed in these instances is clearly the same as that depicted in the painting. The more one is familiar with Munch's work the more specific shots evoke or consciously allude to paintings or lithographs, many of which (*The Dead Mother and the Child, Tingel-Tangel, Music on Karl Johan Street, Tête-à-Tête, Friday Evening, Girls on the Bridge*, etc.) are not even seen in the film. These visual references are not even limited to Munch's paintings. The entire sequence depicting the humiliating venereal-disease inspection of Line Pedersen, a young prostitute, is modeled on Christian Krohg's painting, *Albertine*.

Watkins also avoids the more traditional methods of presenting paintings in a film about an artist. There are few long lingering pan shots over the surface of paintings, and instead, the camera concentrates on specific details of carefully selected works to strengthen further the development of Watkins' key themes. Although between thirty and forty different canvases are seen in various contexts throughout the film, one must admit that Watkins, given the length and scope of the film, uses the paintings of Munch and other artists sparingly. This, according to the director, was done quite consciously as part of his protest against the "limited way" that art historians deal with artists. There are a number of references (Rodin, Klinger,

Gauguin, Vallotton, Gustave Moreau, etc.) throughout the film to artistic influences on Munch, but this aspect is deliberately downplayed. Rather the emphasis is on the effect of Munch's personal life on his work—as a kind of balance against the view that an artist's output is chiefly explainable through a study of artistic influences. "Most art historians have to take an aesthetic or intellectual viewpoint," according to Watkins. "They never, never, never try to go into the soul of an artist. Of course, you really can't go inside the soul of a man; you can only go into your own soul in the end. That's why this film is extremely personal."[7]

According to legend, when an ancient Kalmuk Tartar high priest died, the person next in rank set about composing his "biography" in the following manner: "first he burns his hero's body to ashes, and then moistening the ashes with water and his own saliva, he kneads them into a dough—'the sacred dough'—and then kneads the dough into a statuette, taking care that the statuette's face shall suggest as far as possible a kind of amalgamated expression representing both artist and subject."[8] Watkins' investigation of "the soul" of Munch through self-analysis was possible, in part, because Watkins and Munch are "soul mates," and the result of his efforts, *Edvard Munch*, like the Kalmuk statuette, is an accurate amalgam of both artists.

In "*Edvard Munch*: A Director's Statement," Watkins describes his first encounter with Munch's paintings and graphics in 1968. "I remember sensing a very strong connection with Munch's experience, on the most personal level—sexual fear and inhibition, need, yearning, a remembrance of brief moments lost for ever, and half a life of aching, and longing . . . and from that moment, I knew that I would make a film about this man, because, in that way, I knew that I would also be making a film about myself." Indeed, as Watkins began to study Munch in depth, he began to realize the myriad ways in which their lives touched each other. Further on in his "Director's Statement," Watkins writes, "The main strength of Munch's tension, though, lies within his deepest sexual and personal needs, and of my relationship to these needs I prefer to write nothing, believing that much lies open and exposed in the film." The author must respect Watkins' wish not to discuss detailed specifics of his private life, but still the personal dimension is too significant to be reduced simply to the generalization that Watkins shared affinities with Munch.

While Watkins did not undergo Munch's childhood acquaintance with sickness and death, the insecurity of Munch's early life finds its parallel in Watkins' own wartime experiences as a child, and in both cases this constant exposure to the uncertainties of life helped to shape attitudes and artistic outlooks. Like Munch's father, the filmmaker's parents objected to many of their son's views and to his choice of profession. As a young man, Munch sought for meaningful relationships and connections with others, and Watkins has done the same – often with equally painful results. Watkins also possesses, like Munch, a tension within his personality between a reserved, controlled exterior and a churning flow of passionate emotions just below the surface. In fact, it is probably because of their similar experiences in these areas that so much of their work deals specifically with the problems of human communication.

Like Munch, who spent most of his middle years in self-exile, Watkins has been forced to do the same in order to find even remotely sympathetic intellectual climates for his work and funding for his films. The nature and language of critical attacks brought against the work of Edvard Munch during most of his lifetime also bear striking comparison to much that has been said about Watkins and his films. For instance, Munch's October, 1895, exhibition at the Blomquist Gallery in Christiania (now Oslo) was attacked by the newspaper *Aftenposten* as being "the hallucinations of a sick mind." The newspaper *Morgenbladet* stated "so much nonsense and ugliness . . . low and repulsive . . . crude and shrieking hideousness," and its editor suggested that "an empty gallery would be the best way to control these extravagances." The February 3, 1966, issue of the *Manchester Evening News* expressed rather similar attitudes about Watkins' *The War Game*. "The film is the most sickening in the world today and one the public should never see." Indeed, most of the adjectives used in unfavorable reviews of Watkins' work ("paranoid," "hysterical," "tasteless," "offensive," etc.) were applied to Munch's paintings by the critics of his day.

It is not enough, however, simply to compare the criticisms brought against the work of both men. Beyond this, there are even similarities in their artistic sensibilities. Much of the art of Peter Watkins and Edvard Munch depends on the development of unresolved tensions and on the attempt, no matter what the consequences, to remain true to their own feelings. Each in his own unique way seeks what Munch calls "an art which takes hold and affects one," and each believes that his art is neither morbid nor sick. Surely, one could apply Munch's description of his achievement in painting ("a sound release . . . a healthy reaction which one can learn from and live by") to all of Watkins' films—but most notably to his film biography of Munch. According to Watkins, a "primary" level of the film comes from "my own feelings, twisting in and out of what I perceived to be Munch's feelings. Or rather, let me say, I never tried to make decisions about what Edvard Munch 'felt'—at a very early stage, I realized the utter futility (and arrogance) of this—instead, I tried to fuse my feelings about my childhood, my own sexual experience, my own work, into a recreation of various events that occurred to Munch." On one level, Watkins' film is a therapeutic "sound release" for himself, but it is, of course, also much more than this.

As in *Punishment Park*, Watkins tried, in his film biography of Munch, to provide a framework which involved his nonprofessional actors to the degree that they were allowed to express some of their own attitudes and emotions. Unlike his films set in the future, there were limiting factors, most notably physical appearance, which affected the casting of this film. To help solve his difficulties Watkins placed notices in Norwegian and Swedish newspapers in an effort to locate individuals who physically resembled Edvard Munch, Inger Munch, Christian Krohg, Stanislaw Przybyszewski, Hans Jaeger, and August Strindberg. Since there were fewer historical guidelines for Mrs. Heiberg and many of the woman from the Christiania Boheme, Watkins allowed himself greater flexibility for these characters. Obviously, looking for the right facial type was important in all cases, but Watkins' approach to selecting the cast was largely intuitive, and final decisions were often made only after discussions with individuals about their own attitudes and their reactions to the situations encountered by the characters in the film. On occasion, intuition and coincidence produced especially fortunate choices. Alf-Kåre Strindberg was selected to play August Strindberg even before Watkins learned his surname and that he was a direct descendant of the Swedish playwright.

Coincidence was even more astonishing given the background of Gro Fraas who portrayed "Mrs. Heiberg" and Geir Westby who played Munch. Gro Fraas was selected after she accompanied a friend who was being interviewed for the role. Her own personal relationships with men included a painful divorce, and she seized upon the opportunity to express some of her feelings about male-female relations in the film. Geir Westby, who bears a striking physical resemblance to the young Munch, was also similar to the artist in less obvious ways. He is an introverted young man who, as a child, suffered frequent asthma attacks. At the time of the filming, he was an amateur artist who was involved in a relationship with an older woman, and since then, in part as a result of working on the film, he has become a full-time art student.

In preparing his actors for sequences to be filmed, Watkins discussed the known characteristics of the people being portrayed, but he still allowed for actors to express their own sentiments. Throughout the film he tried to fuse together levels of what he calls "pure recreation," "mixed recreation," and the "feelings of the actors":

> Most of what I do is defined by lots of discussions with the people in the cast which goes on levels of both talking about the characteristics, as far as we know them, of the person being recreated, plus a lot of talk about the person–himself or herself–who is going to be playing the part. When I say playing the part, I mean being a mixture of somebody else and themselves which is usually very integral, because I never make any attempt to make somebody, somebody else. I thrash out scenes with people. For example, in the scenes where Munch and Mrs. Heiberg talk to each other, I would simply work with both people playing their parts. . . . There were instances where it was known what Munch said to her and she to him. I would discuss these with them and see how they felt about them. Sometimes I'd actually try and get them to recreate dialogue that actually occurred, though I pointed out to them that whatever Mrs. Heiberg said was from a very biased source, since everything was written by Munch. So, very often, some of the scenes were worked out by the two human beings concerned. . . . What we did in the film was to find a very strong woman who in her personality had some similarities to Mrs. Heiberg, but who was also strong in her own way. So we usually got her to deal in the film with events, how she as a woman would have

dealt with them had she been there then and how she was now. It is a complex form of living history which you watch in the film.[9]

With Oda Lasson (Eli Ryg) and the younger woman from the Boheme, Watkins granted his performers even greater liberty. He suggested a general thematic direction, but then allowed them to express their own feelings about marriage and a woman's freedom in a relationship with a man. For Watkins, this approach is more honest than using professional actors and a carefully constructed script. Indeed, he realizes that, to some extent, he is merely replacing one cinematic convention with another, but given his unique theory of history and his quest for "self-involvement" in film, he believes his method of using amateurs and allowing them to express themselves is essential in a medium which encourages conformity in directorial styles, praises an actor's cultivation of counterfeit emotion, and lulls the audience into a condition of passivity.

As the author has indicated throughout this study, Watkins' "self-involvement" does not stop with himself or with his nonprofessional actors. His cinematic experiments attempt to break down the artificiality of conventional cinema and to lower the barriers that usually exist between subject and viewer—in order to engage members of the audience as individuals who must also participate in the film experience. His innovative editing, his convoluted narrative structure with its deliberate loose ends, and his expressionistic use of sound and color combined with realistic lighting and camera techniques all push in this direction, but in *Edvard Munch*, the most obvious device is the staring characters who look directly at us, the audience, not just in interviews but throughout the film.

Of course, this device exists in all of Watkins' films but nowhere else with the relentlessness found here. This emphasis is easily understood, since Munch himself used exactly the same device to create jarring emotional effects in the viewer of such paintings as *Self-Portrait with Burning Cigarette, Angst, Jealousy, The Voice,* and most notably *Death in the Sickroom*. In this last painting, for instance, the emotional states resulting from the death of Munch's sister cannot be communicated among the family members who look away from each other, but Inger, Munch's sister, directly confronts the viewer in an attempt to make him understand and, therefore, share her grief. Reinhold Heller even suggests that at times the completion of certain Munch paintings "is in the eyes of the viewer." *The Voice*, sometimes called *Summer Night's Dream*, depicts a young girl, dressed in white, standing in the woods near a lake. It is midsummer, and a phallic-like reflection of the moon is cast on the lake. In his analysis of this painting, Heller first quotes Franz Servaes, who consulted with Munch about the meaning of the painting, and then presents his own description of this adolescent girl's ambiguous pose which represents both "sexual self-display and doubtful withdrawal." This tension is crucial to all of Munch's work, but for Heller the most fascinating aspect of the painting is the fact that "the girl stares temptingly" at the viewer "as she feels the physical changes and desires of puberty. The viewer is her first suitor."[10] In these paintings and Watkins' film, we are totally involved, directly spoken to, as we look into the character's eyes: eyes which serve as a bridge between their responses and similar feelings within ourselves. In Watkins' film, many characters stare out at us expectantly, but Munch does so in nearly every shot, aside from those when he is talking directly to another character. Throughout the film, Munch is presented as an introverted individual, and this eye contact with the audience provides both crucial non-verbal clues as to his emotional state and an essential empathetic link with the viewer. Unlike the conventional film portraits of artists in *Lust for Life* (1956), *The Moon and Sixpence* (1942), and *Moulin Rouge* (1952) where the artist is pictured as a victim of some strangely fated madness and his life is romanticized into an artist-outsider-criminal syndrome, Watkins shows Munch very much as "one of us"—a man with fears and anxieties isolated in a repressive, hypocritical society, a man whose temperament should not be separated from his work or his social environment. For Watkins, the fact that Munch is still viewed by many art historians and members of the public as an eccentric, an odd outsider, reveals "so much about the way our society regards talking about relationships and feelings. Somehow Munch and what happened to him is like a small allegory for the history of our culture."[11]

Munch was born on December 12, 1863, and died on January 23, 1944. During his long life, he worked continuously, often painting themes and images which preoccupied him as a young man in the 1880s and 1890s. After a nervous breakdown in Copenhagen in 1908, Munch returned to Norway and purchased an estate in Ekely, near Oslo, where he spent the remainder of his life. At his death, he bequeathed all the works in his possession (1,200 paintings, 4,500 drawings, 18,000 prints, and six sculptures) to the city of Oslo, which finally opened the Munch Museum in 1963.

In his film, Watkins ignores any reference to Munch's life after 1908 and concentrates instead on his most significant period as an artist: the eleven-year span from 1884 to 1895 which includes his affair with "Mrs. Heiberg," the death of his father and brother, Peter Andreas, his association with Hans Jaeger and August Strindberg, and the beginning of his work in graphics. Narrow as this focus is, it allows the viewer a richer, more comprehensive understanding of Munch than could have been achieved in the usual birth to death biographical format. Watkins does not limit himself strictly to this eleven-year period of the artist's life; rather these years are merely the "present" for Munch in the film. The "past" is obviously the numerous intercut isolated images, sequences, and nonsynchronous sounds depicting Munch's childhood and "the black angels" (illness, insanity, and death) that constantly accompanied him. The "future" is what happened to Munch after the events depicted in the film take place—specifically his further unsuccessful relationships with women and his placing himself into a Copenhagen psychiatric clinic in 1908. Even on this fundamental level, however, Watkins never offers a simplistic "see the child—see the man" portrait. The past was with Edvard Munch too strongly for that kind of treatment; also, the film's dense texture and intricate structure would not allow for such an approach. The images and sounds of disease, death, and guilt from Munch's childhood do not simply intrude into the so-called present of the film. Some images are free-floating; others form suggestive links with visuals from the recent past or present, and, in turn, repeat and build constantly varying patterns of associations.

Even Watkins' interview technique and his use of the narrator function in merging past, present, and future. In the film, a number of individuals are queried by an off-camera interviewer. Frequently, and especially with Munch's brother Peter Andreas, his sister Inger, and Aunt Karen, the viewer has no idea at what period in time or in exactly what context these figures are being questioned. As such, their presence never seems strictly bound to the past. Watkins also unorthodoxly lingers his camera on the faces of these figures long after they have finished talking, often even while the sounds of a new sequence overlap, in order to suggest that these people were constantly with Munch and to strengthen the psychological effect of their statements on the audience.

For Watkins, much of Munch's artistic output exhibits a portending of things to come—a forboding of the future in terms of growing alienation or perhaps even the world wars which have ravaged our century. As a result, the narrator of the film keeps pace with the years, not simply to provide details of the social, political, and economic milieu in which Munch lived, but to suggest the artist's sensitivity to the future. The events mentioned by the narrator are not as random as they might at first appear. The steady growth of German military strength is carefully traced, and references to the invention of the machine gun, the birth of Adolf Hitler, and the United States' acquisition of Pearl Harbor should trigger associations in any audience. Watkins further alludes to Munch's forward perspective by frequently juxtaposing the narrator's observations, especially those of military significance, with Munch's growing alienation and terror of nature. Thus, for instance, remarks about the kaiser, the Triple Alliance, civil war in Chile, and widespread famine in Russia are immediately preceeded by Munch writing in his diary about seeing "the flaming sky like blood" and feeling "a great endless scream through nature."

Watkins did make an outline for *Edvard Munch*—a type of loose, fragmented script which overlapped images, dialogue, and quotations from the diary, and he even occasionally referred back to this document when he was editing the nearly fifty hours of footage that had been shot. Still, this outline did not determine the film's structure. According to Watkins, he does not work along one single line:

It's extremely important you realize that. . . . The way I work is like the film itself. And I'm fusing together all the different levels all the time. . . . Superficially, the film has a kind of progression of the years, but, of course, it's inordinately mixed up. So much of this is not conscious, which is why I'm not going to disturb and formalize the process by which I created that, which was very often an entirely subjective experience. I refuse to put that into rule books. I refuse to lay it out so anyone else can analyze it.[12]

While Watkins may be unable to explain the specifics of why he used four levels of sound in a particular sequence rather than three or two levels, or why he intercut footage of a beer-hall juggler exactly where he did so, this does not mean that there are not any conscious patterns and motifs or that there is not a rationale for the shifting levels of time in the film. Often form reflects content in Watkins' film about Munch. Like Munch's paintings, Watkins' film pushes beyond the confines of external reality in order to reveal narrative development. Also, Watkins' imagery and editing create patterns which reinforce, not simply how Munch characteristically mingled love and death, but how his personal experiences served as the basis for his formulations about the universal dimensions of his chosen theme. The love-death dichotomy is just one of many perceived by Watkins as existing in Munch, his time, and ours, and thus the entire film moves back and forth between extremes on all levels: social, economic, artistic, religious, and most significantly emotional. As such, every position presented in the film is merely one proposition in an ongoing dialectic—a dialectic that gets amazingly complex with each new layer presented. Like *Punishment Park* and all of Watkins' later films, *Edvard Munch* does not supply solutions; it provides a greater understanding of the self and of a particular situation or problem. Those Marxist critics who have attacked the film for "the unfulfilled promise of historical criticism, implied by the opening structure of the film,"[13] do not really understand the nature of the dialectical process which occurs in this work. They are simply relating to the political-social counterpointing of the Norwegian proletariat, enduring the ravages of child labor and working eighteen hours a day in wretchedly unsafe conditions, with the fashion-conscious bourgeoisie strolling on the Karl Johan. What these critics fail to perceive is that Watkins' dialectic process does not stop at the social, political, or economic level. It entails the counterpointing of tensions between Munch and his family, between his family and the Christiania Boheme, between the Boheme and other artists with whom Munch as-

Munch at work on *The Sick Child*.

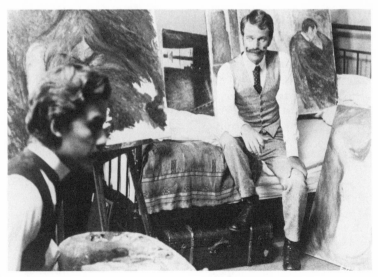

Munch at work in a hotel room.

sociates, between male and female, between contradictory emotional states within himself—the list could be continued almost indefinitely. The constant juxtaposition of visual aspects in *Edvard Munch* is also further reinforced by the multilevel sound tracks which often combine layers of sound associated with contradictory emotions and by the narrator, who often engages in ironic juxtaposition. For instance, near the end of the film, the narrator follows his description of Munch suffering a nervous breakdown in 1908 and placing himself in a Copenhagen psychiatric clinic with the following statement: "At the same time, Munch is to be notified that he has been made a Knight of the Royal Norwegian Order of St. Olaf."

There is no abandonment of the dialectical process in *Edvard Munch*. If anything, there is a strenghtening and subtle enrichment of it as the film progresses beyond the direct and unmistakable juxtapositions (the workers and the bourgeoisie, form cuts from Munch's father to Hans Jaeger, etc.) of the opening exposition. Even the cut from the hands of Munch's father in prayer while his wife is dying to a close-up of "Mrs. Heiberg's" hand clutching Munch's distinctly reflects the painter's preoccupation with interweaving eros and death—as does a cut on the word "death" to an oft repeated shot of "Mrs. Heiberg" about to kiss Munch on the neck. This last shot and a long held close-up of "Mrs. Heiberg" staring at Munch in the dawn light reverberate throughout the film as leitmotifs, and with each repetition, the associations alter slightly through Watkins' juxtaposition of shots. One of the most poignant cuts occurs near the end of the film. Immediately after the arrogant dismissal of Munch's work, "This is not art; it is dirt" (perhaps a more accurate translation of the Norwegian would be "shit") by the pompous editor of *Morganbladet*, Watkins cuts to "Mrs. Heiberg" looking at Munch as a reminder of the intensity of Munch's feelings and their importance in his art.

Just as Munch's painting *Love and Pain*, now called *The Vampire*, is far more ambivalent than Stanislaw Przybyszewski's renaming of it suggests, Watkins' shot of Munch with "Mrs. Heiberg" hovering over him about to kiss his neck balances tension and fear with tenderness and longing, and the impact of this shot often depends on the context in which it is placed. For Watkins, this image (which evokes a number of paintings rather than simply reproducing a content of *The*

Vampire) sums up the ambiguity in Munch's relationship with "Mrs. Heiberg." In using it so frequently throughout the film, he attempts "to integrate this woman and Munch's feelings for this woman and this woman's face into both a metaphorical and also an extremely real image for him of life, death, intense joy and intense pain and hurt—and intermingle her with his mother."[14]

Munch's affair with "Mrs. Heiberg" lasted for six years, and it is the source of Munch's complex conception of women, an attitude which the narrator of the film describes in some depth. "The triple aspect of Munch's feelings for Woman—the Temptress, the Devourer, for whom he has both revulsion and a deep longing; the Virgin, the Innocent, for whom he has respect; the Giver of Life, the Mother, the Sacrificer, for whom he has compassion. The complexity of Munch's suffering—of his art—is that each of these three images, for him, are one and the same woman." For Watkins, this abstract woman was personalized for Munch in "Mrs. Heiberg." Therefore, Munch's relationship with her forms the central core of the film, and an expanding effect, much like circular ripples in a pond after being pierced by a stone, exists as a further layer on top of the dialectical structure already discussed. In the film, the audience encounters various glimpses of "Mrs. Heiberg" long before she is identified or even linked with Munch, and the first time they actually saw each other on a boat going down the Christiania fjord to the village of Borre is not presented until later in the film when Munch first attempts to work in graphics. Shots of "Mrs. Heiberg" are intercut with Åse Carlsen and Miss Drefsen as Munch attempts to establish other relationships, with the death of his sister Sophie, with his visit to a brothel in Berlin, and with his self-sacrificing mother. Watkins even suggests through his editing that, although Dagny Juell is the external model for *Madonna*, "Mrs. Heiberg's" presence infuses the painting. The ripple effect is further emphasized in that the feelings (longing, loathing, tranquillity, jealousy, emptiness, and despair) aroused as a result of Munch's love for this woman are mirrored in the relationships of those around him. Parallels abound throughout the film, and they are often reinforced by using the same spatial relationships within the frame for different characters in similar circumstances. All the characters in the film are unique individuals, but their situations are often interchangeable. Munch complains about "Mrs. Heiberg" ignoring him to a patient Hans Jaeger, who serves as Munch's surrogate father, but Munch soon finds himself in the role of sympathetic listener when Jappe Nilssen complains that he can no longer put up with the treatment accorded him by Oda Lasson, Hans Jaeger's former mistress.

As the film progresses toward its conclusion, Watkins claims that he "deliberately let the complexity grow more and more . . . to reflect his [Munch's] torment."[15] One of these particular moments of "torment" occurs in the German dance-hall sequence near the end of the film. This sequence not only suggests the inspiration for the painting *The Dance of Life*, but it reinforces Munch's major thematic concern in *The Frieze of Life*. Munch himself has written at some length about being seated in a Paris dance hall, when the sights and sounds of the singers and musicians, the smoke, and the dancing couples became a vision of life:

> I felt the need to do something. I felt it would be easy, anything would shape under my hands as if by magic. This is what I would present: a strong naked arm, a strong brown neck, a young woman putting her head against a burly chest. I wanted to paint all this as I was seeing it just now, but in a blue haze. This couple at the moment when they were not just themselves but only a link in a chain of a thousand generations. . . . I should like to make a number of such pictures. No longer shall I paint interiors, and people reading or women knitting. I shall paint living people who breathe and feel and suffer and love.[16]

In Watkins' film, the source of Munch's vision is not simply the unknown dancers who do not look at each other, but all the feeling, suffering, and loving people from his past. The montage of short shots, possibly arranged to complement the frantic rhythms of the can-can music and the boisterous gaiety of the beer-hall crowd, do not simply serve as recall images in order to make clear how much Munch's past remained forever with him. Through form cutting and careful manipulation of rhythm, the images swirl, blur, and blend together. It almost becomes impossible to tell exactly where the cut occurs, and as a result, identities momentarily dissolve. Dagny Juell, dancing with Munch at "The Black Pig," turns around just as

Watkins cuts to a shot of the similar whirling movement of a can-can dancer. Close-ups of Strindberg and Przybyszewski are immediately replaced by shots of customers' faces in the beer hall. A kicking leg becomes a thin gouge explosively carving a woodcut. Close-ups of lithographs, etchings, and woodcuts (many including images that were first created in his paintings) are also intercut to suggest the psychological process behind Munch's creativity, since the preceding sequence carefully detailed the physical process of making graphics. In other instances, most notably the painting of *The Sick Child* and *Melancholy* (also known as *Evening* or *The Yellow Boat*), Watkins interrelates Munch's techniques and the pain that the pictures were about, so that the audience comes to understand the relationship between the psychological and professional process—the meaning and reasons for the techniques used.

These montages of images from the past and present, like so many others in the film, are not meant to imitate the dynamics of memory; they are not flashbacks in the traditional sense or the literal depiction of the images floating through Munch's mind. Occasionally in the film, we are placed in Munch's subjective perspective, such as when he returns home after the first critical onslaught against *The Sick Child*. The distorting wide-angle lens and the reeling, almost stumbling, camera express cinematically the depths of his alienation and sense of rejection. Also, with such statements as "memories and images stored over twenty years are about to burst forth" and "he struggles to remember, and struggles to forget," the narrator seems to suggest that, at times, the visual images in the film attempt to mirror those passing through Munch's mind. Watkins, however, is careful not to present images from Munch's past to complement these words.

Watkins' complex montage of sounds and images from the past and present are part of an attempt to delineate the psychological process through which Munch creates his art, and Munch's process of painting—blurring details, blotting out sections, distorting form, and exaggerating line, perspective, and color to reflect his own personal vision—is also akin to Watkins' process. Perhaps because Watkins is so intensely interested in process rather than the achievement of an inviolable, "perfect" film, he was able to reedit his original three

and a half hour version of the film into a two hour and forty-
seven minute cinema release version and still feel that he in
no way compromised himself or the film:

You've only got to make one cut or start to cut and you have immediately displaced the whole construction. So you are forced with
the necessity of recutting [the entire film], and obviously I didn't do
that for the sake of doing it. I only did it because I felt I could advance
the film. If you are going to shorten the film, the film has to change
somewhat. It means that somebody seeing the cinema version as opposed to the television version will just get slightly different things
out of it at times: slightly more emphasis than they would have in the
other version or slightly less emphasis. Because this is such a complex subject, that doesn't matter. I mean who is to say that one is
better than the other? There are so many issues and tangents and
subtangents.[17]

When Watkins recut the cinema version of *Edvard Munch*,
he also reconsidered and rearranged much of his complex
sound montage. Before the shooting of the film began, however, he was unaware of the degree to which he would employ
multiple tracks for sound overlays. He always works closely
with sound technicians, and for this film, he stressed the
necessity of recording a great deal of atmosphere noise. Special attention was given to recording the sounds of Munch at
work. Frequently the recording microphone (with maximum
gain) was placed a fraction of an inch from the back of the
canvas, and the sound recordist was expected to follow the
movements of the brush or pencil across the canvas. The resulting sound, often kept at top level and mixed with up to
three other tracks, complements extreme close-ups of brush
work, palette knife, or gouge. The effect can be staggering as
Munch scores deep into the canvas with the end of his brush
or scratches into a copper plate with a drypoint needle. Watkins also frequently orchestrates these sounds to underscore
or to contrast with dialogue, images, or nonsynchronous
sounds. For instance, the narrator's discussion of Munch's
techniques in painting *Melancholy* is accompanied by close-
up shots and appropriate, exaggeratedly loud sounds. This
painting is Munch's first attempt to depict jealousy, "and not
merely the event of jealousy, but its psychology and innermost
quiver." At the word "quiver," the charcoal streaks across the
canvas with a harsh, audible shudder.

Throughout the film, Watkins uses sound in an expressionistic manner. Background tracks, often the sound of crying or the cries of sea gulls, run over into new scenes and continue during the commentary, only to be cut off suddenly. Watkins also frequently just removes the music track where the image is cut without any consideration for the beat of the music. "Even on the most basic technical level, it's extremely unusual to cut tracks off like I do. I just chop off the soundtracks. You know, I don't kind of wrap the soundtrack up nicely with the music. . . . I believe very much in totally removing all the kind of normal politesse of technique. So to suddenly have an extremely rich track and to suddenly almost kind of take the audience over a cliff so they drop into a well of silence is extremely tense."[18] Up to three tracks of nonsynchronous sounds are often combined with the sync track and played at exactly the same sound level. The result is that layers and layers of Munch's past experiences flood the viewer, and when these ever-changing complicated sound patterns are combined with a constant barrage of disparate shots, the viewer experiences a level of complexity perhaps unmatched in the history of cinema.

Watkins also worked closely with his cameraman, Odd Geir Saether, who, since a tripod was used only to photograph artwork, shot ninety-eight percent of the film with a hand-held 16mm Arriflex. Although Saether had worked for years with Norsk Rikskringkasting production crews and was thoroughly professional, Watkins asked him to film in ways totally new to him, and it took some weeks before he was able to respond creatively. For instance, Watkins did not want the various takes of a scene to be alike. According to Saether, Watkins "wanted the takes to be quite different so that he could intercut between different takes. Well, what soon happened was that each day of working was so fatiguing that, as a matter of fact, I just forgot about these things he had been talking about, and I fell back on routines that were more normal to me." Since the lab took over a week to process the rushes, it took some time for Watkins to realize what was happening. After three weeks of shooting, two weeks were set aside for screening. During this period, Saether came to realize that Watkins, "who was scaring the hell out of me, had understood so much about this medium that no one else ever could. During those weeks, I came to see these scenes as he did, and I could hear his cues before they came."[19]

Saether was given considerable freedom to shoot "candid moments" throughout the production, but Watkins was especially concerned with the framing of close-ups and the placement of figures in the frame. In many instances, he sought to recreate Munch's spatial tension between forms where the air surrounding figures almost seems to attack them. Additionally, like Munch, he presented close-up images with active background figures in order to create yet another type of tension and an animated milieu.

Perhaps the most striking visual effect achieved by Watkins and Saether was a cinematic equivalent for Munch's "nervous dissolving treatment of color." Watkins had experimented with indirect lighting and the desaturation of color in his previous films, but the task of using color, like Munch, in a totally expressionistic manner presented numerous difficulties. Something of the desired effect could be achieved by varying the grain of the image and by using filters and indirect lighting, but this was not enough.

In the film, Sigurd Bødtker mentions that Munch discovered in *The Iliad* that the Greeks regarded death as blue. Whether this is the major way in which Munch conceived of blue is difficult to answer, but critic Franz Servaes, as early as 1893, noted that he frequently created mood, not through composition, but through color, "specifically Munchean blue-violet . . . his beloved mystical deep blue."[20] In order to create atmosphere and mood, Watkins wanted to capture something of the strange, almost insubstantial, quality suggested by Munch's use of blue. By accident during the testing of various film stocks, indoor film mistakenly marked as daylight type was used without a corrective filter. According to Saether, "When we got into the screening room with this, Peter screamed, 'That's how we want it!' Because the light was extremely heavy, extremely bluish, and shooting had been done with a stock for artificial light, it came out extremely blue."[21]

Although *Edvard Munch* is Watkins' most innovative film, his most personal, and his least controversial (certainly in terms of subject matter), it is a film which has brought him considerable frustration—not in the course of completing the project itself, but because of NRK's reaction to possible future projects and what could almost be called the indirect suppression of the film after its initial showing.

Although some critics complained about the length of the film and the use of modern Norwegian dialect by the actors, the initial critical reactions in Norway and especially Sweden were nothing short of extraordinary. Bertil Behring in *Kvällsposten* not only called *Edvard Munch* a "great artistic achievement" but praised the fact that Watkins, "an Anglo-Saxon, . . . has pentrated into the world of Edvard Munch with tremendous intensity and will for knowledge." In *Expressen*, Hemming Sten indicated that the film was an instant classic, and Sonja Wallander (*Värmlands Folkblod*) claimed that with his depiction of Munch, Watkins' "distinctive talent has come fully into its own." Even Lars Löfgren, production head of Sveriges Radio's second channel, wrote to Watkins shortly after the telecast: "It is unbelievable what a great impact your film has made on the press and on the audience. Of course, I knew that I liked it and that many others would love it just as much, but I did not have the faintest idea that such a great audience in Sweden would take the film to the heart and love

An exhibition of Munch's paintings.

it so much. I have every day been involved in talks about the
film and people and papers are constantly calling to ask us
when we will be showing the film again." Later in the letter,
Löfgren mentions a discussion with Ingmar Bergman, who not
only liked the film but said it was the work of a genius.

With this kind of response to the Munch film, Watkins proposed that he join NRK

in order to foster various important elements that I think I have
developed with the Munch film. . . . I would like to use the making of
. . . films to help train and develop young Norwegian cameramen,
designers, sound technicians, and production assistants, in what I
feel is the most relevant way possible—by engaging them directly in
productions in the field. I think that the stimulus and training involved here could be important for Norwegian television, also. Finally, I think that it is vital to stress the necessity for a greater awareness of the public, and of their needs, than at present seems to exist in
much of Western television. I would hope to be able to help those
members of your organization who wished to move in this direction. . . .[22]

NRK responded by saying that no new hiring was con-
templated, and Sveriges Radio indefinitely delayed making a
final decision after Watkins made a similar request to them.
These negative responses may have resulted from the fact that
he was a foreigner, from jealousy over the success of *Edvard
Munch*, from an adverse reaction to his intense seriousness,
and / or from dislike and possible fear of his ideas about the
role of media.

The issue of Watkins' foreigness frequently emerged as part
of the reason for the cancellation of several projects that were
proposed for production after the completion of *Edvard
Munch*. Rolf Riktor, Head of NRK's Children and Youth Department, for instance, dropped a film that Watkins had
planned about the relationship between young people and
their parents in a typical Norwegian home located in the sub-
urbs of Oslo, because the director was not a Norwegian: "We
think such 'close-ups' of young people in particular parts of
this country, due to a necessity for knowing the cultural backgrounds, the language, etc. should be dealt with by Norwegian
authors / directors."[23]

The jealousy and resentment within NRK over the Munch
film not only affected Watkins' chances to join the organiza-

tion but also the job assignments for those who worked on the film. One especially talented technician wrote to Watkins some time after the telecast of the film: "It seems I have done my last job for NRK. The jealousy and envy of the staff in the film dept. seems to have reached a peak after the showing of the Munch film, and they are now pressing very hard on the administration to have a guarantee against free-lancers 'getting the best jobs.' And that goes for you too since you had the nerve to edit the film yourself."

In August, 1975, the author discussed Watkins' work with Lars Löfgren in Stockholm. Although full of praise for the films that Watkins had made in Scandinavia, Löfgren noted that Watkins' intensity, seriousness, and intellectuality frightened people. Just a few days before, however, a technician from Sveriges Radio had said in an interview that the fear of Watkins came from senior officials who were concerned about the effects of his ideas.

Perhaps Watkins expected too much from the Scandinavians. Certainly, no one can deny them the right to refuse him a regular position in their broadcasting corporations. What is difficult to understand and impossible to justify, however, is the lack of support given by these networks to *Edvard Munch*, when it promised to provide considerable financial gain and recognition on the world market.

Shortly after the first telecast of the film, NRK informed Watkins that a distant member of the Munch family objected to some references in the film. Even though no legal judgment was ever made about the libellous nature of the description in question, Watkins was told that unless he altered the material, the film would never again be shown in Norway. Although he objected, Watkins made modifications which gained the support of both the Munch Museum and Sveriges Radio. NRK, however, simply censored the entire soundtrack of the sequence and attempted unsuccessfully to pressure Sveriges Radio into using their version for all future telecasts.

After this incident, the Munch film was largely ignored on all levels. Not only was it unscheduled for showing at the 1975 Nordisk Screenings (an important festival in which Scandinavian television films are exhibited to potential buyers from European networks), but it was not even listed in the supplementary catalog of films available. Watkins' angry protests finally resulted in the exhibition of the film to the European representatives, and ironically it became the most successful film at the festival—even outselling Bergman's *The Magic Flute*. Months later when Watkins confronted Orjan Wallquist, controller of SR's second channel, about the reasons why *Edvard Munch* had not originally been included in the Nordisk Screenings, Wallquist simply replied that "there is no point in talking about the past."[24]

There were also problems with the proposed cinema release of *Edvard Munch*. Lars Löfgren had asked that the film be shortened for this purpose, but even after Watkins reedited the television version, no action was taken to blow up the film from 16mm to 35mm. Löfgren suggested that the delay was caused by a lack of finance and by labor problems with Norwegian technicians about their rights and residuals from a cinema release. The financial reason seemed odd, since the television version of the film had just been sold to West Germany, England, Ireland, Yugoslavia, and Poland; and Löfgren's second claim was loudly disputed a few days later by several Norwegian technicians who spoke with the author about their work on the film.

At this same time, when plans for a cinema version of *Edvard Munch* were being discussed by Sveriges Radio in Stockholm, NRK in Oslo destroyed all the original soundtracks of the film and all the quarter-inch tapes which had been used to record the music. When Watkins asked why NRK destroyed material so essential to any enlargement of the film, he was informed that this was "done to clear shelf space."

In the autumn of 1975, plans for the blow up were finally put into operation, but in mid-November, SR and NRK abruptly and unexplainedly ceased all lab work on the cinema version of the film. After a number of fruitless trips to Oslo and Stockholm in an attempt to get the laboratory to begin work again, Watkins finally achieved his goal by threatening to reveal his plight to the press: "I told SR I would get the laboratory rolling by paying for the first installment myself, and immediately appealing for public finance (via the press) or by approaching the film industry. I also told them that if that had to happen, I would immediately take over all distribution of the film."[25]

When the 35mm version was completed in early 1976, Watkins requested SR and NRK submit the film to the Cannes Festival as the official Norwegian entry. NRK refused to do so on the grounds that it did not wish to compete with the Norwegian film industry, even though no other film was being considered as the official Norwegian entry that year. When NRK finally reversed its decision (after further pleas from Watkins and the SR Sales Department), it was too late; the deadline for submission to the festival had passed.

Watkins' fight to gain the widest possible audience for *Edvard Munch* was often frustrating, demeaning, and exhausting, but in the last phases of the battle, he was not alone. Florence Bodin, of SR's TV Export Department, staunchly supported the cinema release of the film, and although decisions of SR executives baffled her as much as they did Watkins, she somehow managed to convince SR to spend 20,000 dollars for the New York opening of the film, on September 12, 1976.

Aside from screenings of the original television version of *Edvard Munch* at the University of Kansas, Utica College, and Mohawk Valley Community College with Watkins present to translate the Norwegian dialogue, only cinema release prints have been shown thus far in the United States. Watkins convincingly argues for the integrity of each version of the film, but it is necessary to distinguish briefly between them. The major advantage of the cinema release version is that the dramatic flow of the first half of the film is substantially increased. In the original version, the exposition is much more detailed, and while some of this information is not absolutely crucial, it is not without importance. The limitations of the Boheme way of life are more readily apparent; the artistic philosophies of Christian Krohg, Fritz Thaulow, and Hans Heyerdahl are explained in more depth, and Hans Jaeger's role as a father figure for Munch becomes especially significant. Also, in the original version, the sections portraying Strindberg and "The Black Pig" crowd are more complex. Strindberg is more fully developed, and the fact that he replaces Jaeger as a major influence on Munch assumes greater importance. The tensions between Munch and his father are richer and more ambiguous in the original. Missing from the cinema release prints, for instance, is a magnificent scene with the Munch family at dinner. Almost as a peace offering, Edvard's father has bought his son a bottle of wine:

DR. MUNCH: Look what I bought for you on Helgelandsmoen, Edvard.

EDVARD: Is it wine? It doesn't look very good.

Slowly the camera zooms into a close-up of Dr. Munch, who stares into the lens with an expression of hurt and rejection. Finally, the last sequence of the film delineates the metaphorical representation of Munch's *The Dance of Life* in a more rhythmically effective manner in the original version, where the images, although quite literal, provide a more satisfying climax to the film.

Still, no matter which version is seen by the public, Watkins' purpose in making *Edvard Munch* remains the same:

There is no single "why" for making this film—the reasons lie buried deep in a complexity of feelings, and needs—but if there is any "reason" needed to justify this film—it is because I knew, instinctively, that Edvard Munch himself—despite endless hardship and personal anguish, despite the acute repressiveness of his background and the social environment in which he worked—remained entirely true to himself, on every level of his existence, and let nothing stand in the way of his self-expression—no matter how much pain, or professional backlash, that self-expression caused him. It is on this level that I have tried to create this film—in recognition of the example that Edvard Munch set for me, and sets for all of us.

Munch's brother, his father, and the model for *The Sick Child*.

One of the shots that Watkins uses as a leitmotif in *Edvard Munch*.

5

Film and Videotape: Recent Scandinavian Projects

AFTER THE COMPLETION of *Edvard Munch*, Watkins remained in Scandinavia to work on free-lance projects for Danmarks Radio and Sveriges Radio and to make a feature film, sponsored in part by the Danish Film Institute.

70-talets Människor (The 70s People)

In April, 1974, Watkins went to Copenhagen to begin work on a film dealing with suicide to be made for Danmarks Radio. The original project, entitled *The Skyscraper*, was to have concentrated on the background to a young woman's attempted suicide. During a four-month period of research and preparation for shooting the film, Watkins changed his concept considerably. Although it still concerned suicide and even depicted the reconstruction of a young girl's attempt to jump off a skyscraper apartment building, this film delved more "into the complexities of modern living in an industrialized society in the West, with its stress, alienation and sense of identity crisis."[1] The reasons for this shift in emphasis stemmed directly from the results of Watkins' research into the rate of attempted suicides in Denmark and from his growing recognition of the vast contradictions between the convivial, jovial exterior of the Danes and their reserve and fear of contact on an emotional level.

Before coming to Denmark, Watkins knew that it had the world's sixth highest suicide rate, and his initial investigation indicated that the number of deaths per year was about twelve hundred. The typical Danish suicide victim is a lonely male in his late fifties or sixties. Although the Danes had efficiently recorded all kinds of information about fulfilled suicides, they

159

Evening Land: *(top) Workers discuss the strike; (bottom) European Common Market defense ministers.*

could answer almost none of Watkins' questions about the number and the makeup of those who attempted suicide. Since poison is employed in over eighty percent of Danish suicides and attempted suicides, Watkins asked the director of the poison ward at Copenhagen's main hospital to conduct research into the backgrounds of those admitted into the city's poison wards during the past year. This study uncovered that about a third of the in-patients were young people between the ages of sixteen and twenty-nine who did not ingest toxic substances or barbiturates by accident. Through the assistance of this same doctor, Watkins also found, just before recording the commentary for the completed film, that the suggested figure for attempted suicides was quite unrealistic:

> We reexamined the figures of in-patients checked into all the poison wards throughout Denmark during one year. We discovered that the total was almost *ten thousand*. The doctor stated that it was hardly likely that more than a very small portion of these were accidental poison cases—and then we looked at each other, and realized that the long-vaunted official ratio for attempted suicides in Denmark was at least 50 or 60% *lower* than it should have been—in other words, that instead of 3,000-4,000, the actual figure was between 7,000-8,000.[2]

While Watkins was engaged in this research, he also placed a notice in Copenhagen newspapers, not necessarily seeking cast members for a film, but trying to contact people who felt anxious about their lives or identities and wished to discuss their feelings. Over three hundred Danes of all ages and social groups responded. Watkins met briefly with these people in large groups. He then held a number of small group discussions for longer periods of time, and finally he met with about thirty or forty people individually for a series of long, personal talks:

> It is very hard, now, to express what I feel about the many hours of intense personal conversations that ensued. I talked about myself, and the Danes did too. . . . Though each of these people talked about extremely personal and individual factors affecting their lives, certain similarities did emerge. One was a sense that many of them had a surfeit of the material society—they had begun to feel, very deeply, that there was something missing from their lives. We discussed this elusive factor a great deal.[3]

Many of the young people in these groups claimed that they were neither taken seriously nor treated as young adults by their parents. Watkins also visited four or five schools in and around Copenhagen, where students, in private discussions, expressed intense feelings of alienation.

These discussions and the fact that many more young people in Denmark attempt suicide than was originally thought drastically changed Watkins' conception of how to make the film that was to become *The 70s People*. From the thirty or forty people with whom he held intense discussions, Watkins selected seven individuals for the film and built up two family units, each reflecting different sets of problems. The first group, which consisted of Mr. and Mrs. Berg and their two children Anne and Claus, was depicted as a formally structured, somewhat sterile, fairly well-to-do, middle-class family. The second group consisted of a mother and daughter and the man with whom the mother now lives in a less than satisfactory relationship. This group, while still firmly middle class, had more financial difficulties than the Bergs. In both families, the principal figures were teenaged daughters. According to Watkins, the women who agreed to portray the daughters had discussed with him at some length their own problems, especially those concerning relationships with parents: "With their permission we stirred some of these into this kind of semifictional, although totally realistic, situation—as a kind of cover. So it could be said that they are not really talking about their own parents, although they know, and I know, and probably their parents have a sneaking feeling that they are dealing with their own life situations."[4] With the individuals playing Mr. and Mrs. Berg, it was more difficult to tell if they were acting out their own life situations, although the woman involved was actually a conservative member of Parliament who readily admitted that she left her own children alone much too often. The adults in the other family, on the other hand, almost turned their roles into something approaching group therapy. The man had recently divorced, and the woman was actually engaged in a relationship parallel to what is depicted in the film.

Watkins also included in the film actual interviews with many of the young people with whom he held discussions as well as reconstructed interviews with a psychologist, school-

teacher, statistician, doctor, television executive, fire brigade
rescue chief, minister, etc. In most instances, he used people
from these professions in the interviews, but in some cases,
especially when the interview was based on encounters with a
number of people, he used an amateur actor and informed the
audience of the nature of the reconstruction.

Like all of Watkins' films, *The 70s People* functions on a
number of complex levels, but its major significance to a
Danish audience has to be the information that it provides
about the probable number of attempted suicides each year.
The image of Denmark as the "ideal" welfare state is further
tarnished by the revelation that the only suicide crisis centers
in the entire country are run by the Danish Folk Church.
These six centers, which are staffed by ministers and volun-
teers, remain open twenty-four hours a day. They receive no
government funds, and there are no comparable government
centers anywhere in the country. One of the Folk Church
ministers ruefully remarks that "you can get state aid for so
many things in this country. Kindergarten schools for example.
But there's no money for our services." At the very end of the
film, an intern who works in the poison ward at Bispebjerg
Hospital in Copenhagen freely admits that only after people
actually try to kill themselves are they able to get government
sponsored counseling. Even the quality of this assistance,
however, is seriously called into question in the film. Vita
Newlin, a young woman who attempted suicide and was
placed under psychiatric care, argues in a number of interviews that she was not really helped in any way while in-
stitutionalized. Most of her time was spent "at what they
called collective therapy, where they were very keen on us
sitting and doing something with our hands, and I wasn't
interested in that. I've never done it at home, and I couldn't really see the point of sitting, knitting ties and things. So I spent
most of my time there drinking coffee and smoking ciga-
rettes." Shortly before the telecast of *The 70s People*, Newlin
succeeded in taking her own life.

While working on his film, Watkins was told by a Danish
friend that because Denmark is such a small country, "we are
terrified of being ignored. We very much want to be talked
about, but, on the other hand, we don't want to be criticized."
Watkins learned the truth of this observation immediately

after the only Danish telecast of *The 70s People*, on September 24, 1975.

The Danish newspapers were ruthless in their attacks on the film. The perennial criticism that Watkins is a foreigner who does not understand the culture was stridently voiced yet again, and thus "the facts" presented in the film were quickly called into doubt. The film was described by one critic as "a pompous fiasco," and the Marxists, who expected a more direct political film, simply dismissed it as "reactionary propaganda." Without much fanfare, the film was then telecast in Sweden and Norway. A brief extract was also shown at one of the Nordisk Screenings, but Danmarks Radio claims that there was little interest in the film. At present, there is some interest in a United States release on the 16mm nontheatrical market, but little is being done about it. Part of the problem stems from a complaint brought by Poul Hartling, the former Danish premier, who objected to the use of television news footage in the film in which he discusses the rising unemployment rate in Denmark. Even without this difficulty, the attitude toward the film at Danmarks Radio is such that foreign distribution will probably not be encouraged. Bjørn Lense-Møller, head of the television drama department, has publicly stated that "while Watkins is a sensitive documentarist, *The 70s People* did not function as well as it should have." For Lense-Møller, the arguments in the film are not as convincing as they might have been because the presentation, "which deals with problems surrounding suicide from the point of view of a person considering suicide," isn't statistically correct.[5]

In his press statement about the film, Watkins indicated that *The 70s People* is "very critical of the human gap in the Danish welfare system—but it is also a film about the Western world in general." Most Danish critics ignored this point altogether, as well as any analysis of the film's aesthetic aspects or its complex structure—except to say that the organization was muddled and that the film was excessively long and boring.

It is almost impossible to present a plot summary for this 127-minute film. To some extent there is a framework involving a loose chronology which allows for the impression of capturing a day in the life of the two families depicted. Also, there are parallel confrontations within each family near the end of the film, but essentially there is no conventional story line.

The daily routines of both families, which were chiefly built up by the actors themselves, are presented in the film in a *cinéma vérité* fashion, with Watkins as narrator even remarking at one point to Mrs. Berg that he and the television crew have been recording in her home for some time. This, however, is just one pattern of development. Watkins takes these domestic scenes and intercuts them with interviews, an incident in which a young woman attempts to jump from an apartment building, a reconstructed police raid on the youth colony of Christiania, footage depicting the lack of recreational areas at a huge dormitory-style apartment complex in a suburb of Copenhagen, the activities of the rescue unit of the fire brigade, etc. In addition to the above examples, Watkins intersperses material taken from television news programs. Henry Kissinger gives a news conference in Copenhagen in which he discusses the possibilities of an arms agreement between Russia and the United States and the chances for peace in the Middle East. Scenes of starving Ethiopian children and footage of riots also appear, as well as extracts from interviews with Premier Hartling and other world government officials.

Watkins directs a scene from *The 70s People.*

Even the narrator supplies statistics and additional information about the world situation.

Some of this intercut material relates directly to suicide, but much of it concerns the stress of modern living. The constant juxtapositions in the film invite the viewer to construct a pattern of organization from this mosaic of images, but there are no obvious, direct corresponding relationships. Rather Watkins "floats" various "fragments of contemporary life" throughout the film in order to depict the social, political, and psychic world inhabited by us all — including potential suicide victims

The film's structure is much looser than *Edvard Munch*, where Watkins constantly expressed his own feelings through intricate sound and visual montages. With *The 70s People*, he slowed the pace and deliberately created an unrhythmed film which makes considerable demands on its viewing audience. Although there are some rapidly paced montages in the film, the average length of his shots is longer than those found in *Edvard Munch*. In *The 70s People*, Watkins instructed those being interviewed to look into the camera when they felt the need to look at someone, and he again has the camera linger on individuals long after they have finished speaking. These moments of silence allow the audience to relate further to the characters, in part because so much emotional information is found in their faces. This technique is especially powerful in the presentation of Anne Berg, Katrine, and Vita Newlin. Watkins also frequently overlays the soundtracks in order to intensify the psychological tensions of the collapsing world he depicts. The bouncy, buoyant voice of Al Jolson, singing "April Showers," "The Anniversary Song," and "Swanee," reverberates throughout the film as a reflection of the merry, fun-loving Danish exterior, while the images of Anne, the concrete suburban city of apartments, and the daily family routines reflect the sad interior reality of endless monotony and growing alienation. The use of Jolson as a counterpointing device was originally suggested by Jeff McBride, who assisted Watkins in the editing of the film,[6] and while Jolson's songs clearly serve as a classic example of "sugar coating" problems, one can only wonder about the effectiveness of their use in this particularly Danish context.

Although Watkins does attack the bureaucratic structure of the Danish welfare state in *The 70s People*, his chief concern is with the sense of alienation found throughout society, and especially in the relationships between parents and children. In the last section of the film, most of the cross-cutting and interviews focus on this particular aspect. The narrator notes that during the shooting of the film, a Danish television producer asked why the film was being made in the manner it was: "Why are you talking to young people?" A schoolteacher looks into the camera lens to discuss her disturbing experience with the parents of a twelve-year-old boy. The parents do not want to hear about her difficulties with their son; they simply give her permission to hit him and add, "We do at home if he doesn't behave properly." A statistician discusses the tendency in Denmark to treat young adults as children at exactly the time when they are becoming more physically mature. The parents of Marianne, the young woman who tried to jump from an apartment building, at first profess complete surprise at her action but then admit that they have had a number of intense disagreements with her over her boyfriend. Finally, Watkins includes the reconstruction of a police raid on Christiania, an abandoned military complex in Copenhagen, which since 1971 has become the living quarters for many so-called "social losers," especially run-away children. The object of this particular raid is a fourteen-year-old girl, who after being captured, sedated, and transported some two hundred kilometers to a children's institution, runs away again and returns to Christiania three days later.

These examples are set off against confrontations which occur within the two middle-class families that the film has followed in a *cinéma vérité* fashion. Over the traditional dinner of *frikadeller*, Katrine's mother tries to get Fleming, the man she lives with, to talk about their deteriorating relationship. The discussion, however, soon turns to the twelve o'clock curfew for Katrine, which will not be lifted even though she is a member of the dance committee and must clean up after an upcoming dance. Elsewhere, Henrik and Kristen Berg have gone out for the evening. Henrik had promised to play chess with his son, but the game had to be postponed. Even a visit by Kristen's mother does not alter plans, and thus the two children are left to entertain their grandmother. When the parents return home from their respective meetings, they find Claus and Anne still awake and anxious to talk about the fact that their parents are never home. Anne poignantly argues that "we live in a home with lots of furniture and things, but two things are missing in particular." Her father promises to think things over. Watkins then cuts to a montage of a suicide report, television images of starving African children, the climax of the police raid on Christiania, an ambulance, television images of Kissinger, Vita Newlin, and finally he ends the film with the intern from the poison ward arguing that "it is wrong that many young people have to go so far before they can be heard, before they can get help to solve the problems they have."

The 70s People is stylistically different from *Edvard Munch* in some ways, but it uses similar sound overlaying and extends some of the interview techniques employed in the Munch film. Nowhere else in Watkins' work, for instance, are silences used so effectively. *The 70s People* is a major work. Quite probably, next to *Edvard Munch*, it stands as Watkins' most accomplished Scandinavian film, but unfortunately its chances of being distributed, even on the United States 16mm market, remain remote.

Fällan (The Trap)

In 1974, Sveriges Radio in Stockholm invited members of the Swedish public to submit teleplay scripts dealing with the subject of "the future" for possible production. One of the scripts selected was written by Bo Melander, a noted journalist for the *Gothenburg Times*, who took a section from the novel he was writing and developed it into script form. His first intention was to devise two short, counterpointing scripts done as newscasts from the year 2000. One would deal with the desire for materialistic comfort and present-day utopian assumptions about the future, and the other would depict "a world gone to hell." Melander wanted "to have these two—the disaster scenario and the positive scenario—together so people could really recognize the disaster scenario as the most realistic one. On the other hand, the optimistic scenario was what everyone deep inside himself dreamed about, and the contrast between the two should be the thing."[7] SR, however, indicated that they would only accept one script and encouraged Melander to build up the "bleak" script. So Melander focused on the nuclear reactor issue (which was becoming a major political concern in Sweden in 1974) and developed a script about the conflict between two brothers, one of whom is the controller of a radioactive waste station.

While he was finishing the editing of *The 70s People*, Watkins was approached by SR about directing Melander's script. Although the script's subject matter interested him, he disliked its form and its somewhat limited concentration. Therefore, he agreed to direct only if the writer would rework the entire script with him. Since Melander was already familiar with most of Watkins' films, he had no objections to Watkins' stipulation and even indicated that he would have written the script in a totally different manner had he known that Watkins would be the director. In January, 1975, Watkins and Melander overhauled the script in a number of significant ways. Melander increased various details relating to the nuclear issue. Watkins considerably enlarged the original script's fleeting satiric gibes at mass media and created the character of Margareta, the Swedish controller's wife, who plays a pivotal role in the final version of the teleplay. Additionally, through the use of simulated television programs from various Western countries, Watkins allowed for the presentation of multiple aspects of life in the future which reinforce the suppression of freedom depicted in microcosmic form in the film.

Although not originally called *Fällan* (*The Trap*), the new title was appropriate given Watkins' shift in setting to the oppressive home of John, Margareta, and their son, Peter, located some thirty meters below the surface of the earth in the main structure of a nuclear waste station near the West coast of Sweden. It is the eve of the year 2000, and Margareta has invited her husband's brother, Bertil, to celebrate the beginning of the new century with them. With Bertil is Bo, the son of Lars, a third brother, who has been imprisoned because of his "antisocial activities." After rigorous security checks witnessed by Peter and his mother on closed-circuit television, Bertil and Bo finally arrive to have supper with their relatives. During the meal the brothers engage in a bitter discussion about conflicting values, while in the background a television set broadcasts programs from Sweden, Russia, France, East Germany, and the United States. Also present throughout the film is a BBC commentator (played by Watkins), who is never seen, but who frequently talks with the people in the room. He has been assigned to do a feature report on the New Year's Eve celebration of this family which lives underground. As midnight approaches, John announces that he has invited members of his staff and some security officers to a little party. Bertil quickly disrupts the festive mood by arguing that all those present are like caged rats trapped within the confines of a system that they all defend unquestioningly. After the guests leave early, Bertil takes Bo and attempts to leave the station, but he is arrested at a security check point. Bo is also taken away by military policemen. Margareta, who has been watching the events via closed-circuit television, breaks down emotionally and, in the midst of her tears, asks "What kind of life is this we're living?" On the Swedish television channel, State Secretary Robert Andersson then expresses his belief that "the century to come will be a century for humanity, filled with humanity." The final image of the teleplay is a tight close-up of Margareta.

Unlike Watkins' other projects which usually evolved over a lengthy period of time, this one developed quickly. After Watkins and Melander revised the script, they advertised in Stockholm newspapers for people who wanted to be in the film. Unlike the massive response to notices for *The 70s People*, only about thirty-five people responded to ads for *The Trap*. From this group, Watkins selected most of the cast members and began two weeks of intensive work with them. Melander had written carefully phrased exchanges for some scenes; Watkins provided additional dialogue, and, of course, the cast itself was encouraged to make suggestions and, after discussion with the director, to improvise responses. Perhaps because the initial group of interested individuals was so small, Watkins made one of the few serious errors of his career in selecting a cast member. The man chosen to play Bertil, according to Watkins, became increasingly "egocentric" and "eccentric," and finally, just two days before the shooting was to begin, this man was asked to leave the production. With the entire project on the verge of collapse, Bo Melander suggested that he step in and play the part of Bertil. Watkins hesitated, in part because Melander had already refused to play a minor role in the teleplay. Also, according to Melander, Watkins did not see him in the role of Bertil because of the way in which they worked together. "You know I was not that typical guy that was blowing and reacting with arms and legs. But by God, I had to do it, so I tried to do that, and he thought that it was working at least. So there I was."[8]

Four days had been set aside for the shooting of the teleplay, but because Watkins had never worked with video equipment in a large television studio, the first two days were completely lost. For him, "the sheer complexity of the equipment, its size, the time taken to line it up, was a similar experience to being crushed on a soft bed under the weight of an enormous wardrobe."[9]

Unlike *The Gladiators* where he attempted to work within a static style for much of the film, Watkins refused to do so here. Instead, on the third day of the shooting schedule, he insisted that the four cameramen operate their huge, color video cameras in a manner to suggest the hand-held, on-the-spot "newsreel" quality of his film work. At first, the reaction of the crew approached open hostility, since all of them had been rigorously trained to avoid the very things that Watkins was now asking them to do. Also, Swedish television crews work as a "master unit" for only a year, and then they are split up in order to form new units. The rationale behind such a scheme derives from a desire to preserve a particular, overall Sveriges Radio style and from an attempt to eliminate the formation of an "elite" group among technicians. Needless to say, such efficiency also destroys any form of individual expression or originality by entirely eliminating the crew's obligations to be creative. Watkins, however, suddenly foisted part of the burden of creativity on his crew, and some were totally unprepared for their new freedom. Cameramen, for instance, were given the responsibility of selecting images, and Monika Barthelson, rather than Watkins, remained in the control room to select the best shots and to cut from camera to camera.

Watkins "felt it very rewarding" to trust the crew "to respond to the occasion":

I felt that I had handed over part of the normal control that many directors insist on jealously guarding as their inherent prerogative. I felt that I was making allowance for other members of the crew to make dynamic decisions of their own—that they did not need minute-by-minute written notes on when to cut, where to cut, or to whom to cut. In fact, of course, most of us do not need notes or directions at all, in order to make these decisions. Not if we trust each other, not if we all feel that somehow we are working together on a venture that has a common tension and importance . . . somehow, in this experience many of us passed over a threshold of "control" – that we will never again see video production as a technical process of imposing control – but rather that of recording a spontaneous experience in which we can all participate.

By the last day of the shooting most of the crew realized that they were involved in a unique television experience and began to respond enthusiastically to Watkins' demands. Paco Hårleman, who devised innovative methods to achieve indirect lighting effects, welcomed the challenge. For him, "a technician is like a piano to be played upon by the director." While most directors never make demands which test the "instrument" and reveal its range, Hårleman claims that Watkins not only accomplished this feat but, in a mere four days, established a creative, communal atmosphere which was unlike anything that he had previously experienced in his ten-year career as a lighting technician. Egon Blank, the teleplay's technical director, echoed Hårleman's claim that the sense of community and artistic cooperation achieved during the production were unique in SR's history.[10]

While members of the crew were assuming their creative responsibilities during the filming, Watkins remained on the studio floor with the "actors." Various changes with the narrative and the ending of the script were made on the third day of the shooting. Also at that time, Melander proposed that Watkins become the off-screen voice of the BBC interviewer in order to control the tempo, rhythm, and tone of the situation and to stimulate responses and reactions from the cast members. According to Watkins, "the tension of the mixture of tautness and sheer unpredictability was very explosive, and I believe that it released emotions and responses in all of us which might not have occurred under the more usual conditions of control that are imposed in a studio."

Even though things were beginning to come together on the third day, only ten minutes of usable footage were recorded. Aside from problems already discussed, Watkins had to make elaborate arrangements with the sound recordist. Given that videotape does not allow for the complex overlaying of numerous soundtracks in the postproduction stage, Watkins was forced to experiment with most of the overlaying during the actual shooting. This meant, for instance, that the sound from the constantly changing television programs had to be worked in at appropriate moments to serve as background noise and / or commentary on the dramatic confrontations among the various people in John Carlsson's living room.

On the final day of shooting, another fifteen to twenty minutes were filmed before 5:00 P.M. At that time, the cast and crew took a break during which Watkins changed the last section of the teleplay and created a party in which military and civilian personnel gather in the Carlssons' apartment. The cast was told that there would be a complete run-through as a rehearsal, but after the action was videotaped, Watkins insisted on using this material because of the effectiveness of the improvisation. Thus, almost all of the last section was recorded in one lengthy take and later intercut with sections from the television news programs.

The editing of *The Trap* also took place over an astonishingly short period of time, in part because Watkins was committed to a lecture tour, and SR asked that the teleplay be completed before he left, rather than after his return. Lars Löfgren, the SR producer, wanted to broadcast the program as quickly as possible because of its specific relevance to the nationwide debate that was raging over the proposed expansion of nuclear power stations. *The Trap* was telecast on May 14 (just over a month after its completion) and was repeated a few months later. Thus far, outside of Sweden, it has been telecast in Yugoslavia and Italy and screened at a few United States colleges and universities.

Although *The Trap* won the 1977 Prix Futura Award in Bronze, its significance, both in terms of subject matter and the unique method in which it was made, has not been properly acknowledged. Some of the executives at SR disliked the teleplay because of Watkins' use of amateurs, but Stockholm newspapers were generally favorable to all aspects of the production. Perhaps because it dealt directly with the effects of nuclear power on the quality of life in the future, the newspaper *Dagens Nyheter* took the highly unusual step of running an editorial urging its readers to watch the teleplay.

While *The Trap* has been telecast three times in Sweden, Norwegian and Danish television have refused to show it.

Watkins directing scenes from *The Trap*.

Tore Breda-Thoresen, head of the television drama department of Norsk Rikskringkasting, claims that it "was not a very
successful production," and Bjørn Lense-Møller, head of Den-
marks Radio's television drama department, has been even
more emphatic in his dislike. In a June, 1977, radio discussion
about Watkins' work, Lense-Møller said that *The Trap* "was
one of the worst productions Peter has made, if not the worst,"
and in a recent letter to Watkins, he reiterated his view that the
work was not "of a high standard."[11] If these executives are
attempting to measure *The Trap* by the achievements of *Edvard Munch*, they are being most unfair. In some ways, *The
Trap* is a minor Watkins work, but it is clearly of a "standard"
considerably higher than nearly all of the productions telecast
on Scandinavian channels. Breda-Thoreson and Lense-Møller
have failed to recognize the breakthrough that Watkins' teleplay has achieved. His innovations in breaking down the rigid,
impersonal trademarks of Scandinavian television production
seem to have been misconstrued by these executives as rank
amateurism.

The importance of *The Trap*, beyond the process which
evolved in its making, rests chiefly with its attack on media
and its depiction of a complacent world which encourages a
necessary conformity to counterbalance possible threats to security. These threats may be real, but, more likely than not,
they have been created by those in power in order to justify
the curtailment of individual rights and to press for following
the will of the establishment. The nuclear issue is obviously
present in the teleplay, but on the surface level, somewhat like
the decadent pop world of *Privilege*. In fact, given its satiric
tone and its multifaceted assault on media as the central device through which individuals are urged "to pull together"
for the good of society, *The Trap* seems closer to *Privilege* than
to any of Watkins' other films.

In all of his previous, so-called "futurist" films, Watkins
never attempted to change costumes or physical aspects from
the present because, of course, all of his films set in the future
are actually about the present. *The Trap* is no exception to this
generalization. The world in the year 2000 with its détente
between the Russians and the Americans, with its terrorist attacks, with its expansion of nuclear power stations, and its de-

pendence on television is the world of the 1970s and the direction of the near future as seen by Watkins and Melander.

The conflict between the two brothers in *The Trap* provides in microcosmic form alternative value structures available today. The choice is essentially between Bertil's attempt to cling to personal integrity and individual freedoms and John's willingness to sacrifice them for security and materialistic comfort in a period of growing threats and hardships. John justifies his position, in part, by claiming that stability provides freedom:

> The 70s were constantly filled with drivel—you've heard about it and read about it—where people talked about freedom; they talked about democracy, protecting the environment, and such. Now the economy and technology have produced a society in which we've got to have authoritarian rule. And that rule I support because the way things are today the only way is to have a society where those who really know something are in charge. That is what's important.

Bertil, although he seeks his own personal liberty, cannot release himself from the responsibility of caring about people who are starving and dying unnecessarily in third-world countries. For him, technocrats, like his brother, have created a system whereby they try to rule the world by substituting stability and cohesiveness for freedom and democracy. Having no specific solution, however, Bertil, like Steven Shorter, can only assert his self-worth as a human being by raging against the system which denies it. *The Trap* is yet another of Watkins' works which questions the nature of freedom in mid-twentieth-century life and exposes the illusory manner in which our society attempts to convince itself that real freedom still exists even when many rights are "briefly curtailed for the good of all."

Admittedly, since both brothers are fixed in their beliefs about freedom, they simply hurl clichéd rhetoric at each other. The strength of the teleplay, however, is not dependent on the verbal effectiveness with which arguments are presented. In fact, during the heat of the discussions, the improvisations in Swedish were spoken so rapidly that Watkins was not always able to discern exactly what was being said. What mattered more to him was the involvement and passion generated by "ordinary members of the Swedish community" who were engaged in the production and the many layers of tension found within the teleplay. On this second level, for instance, part of the reason for the use of multiple languages both on the television programs and within the dialogue exchanges stems from the fact that it creates an additional layer of tension. Also, of course, the use of numerous languages throughout the teleplay further reflects the universality of the dilemma depicted.

The tensions between the positions of the brothers are further augmented in the portrayal of the two children raised according to conflicting life styles. John's pale-complexioned, wide-eyed son, Peter, "is zapped to hell and back by living this molelike existence. He's extremely intelligent; he's a child of the future."[12] The child knows everything there is to know about nuclear waste, and the constant barrage of information from world-wide television gives him the "proper perspective" on the state of the world. Bo, Lars' son, is about the same age, but he exhibits a crudeness and an emotional depth not found in his cousin. Needless to say, he has not been bombarded by television propaganda since infancy. The crucial character, however, is Margareta, a thoroughly middle-class woman ("In this house we don't swear . . . [and] we don't make crumbs like that") who in no way understands her brother-in-law, but who also seems unfulfilled in her husband's world. According to Watkins, she is "trapped" in a lifeless environment and in a "soulless" marriage. The outcome of the dramatic confrontation in the teleplay is her emotional outburst when Bertil and Bo are taken away by the security police. The tearful questioning about the kind of life we are living mirrors the response that Watkins hopes his audience will have about their own lives as a result of viewing *The Trap*.

The only other character of importance in the teleplay is the BBC interviewer. Although Watkins devised this role chiefly to have input on the studio floor and to exercise some measure of control over the interaction of the characters during long takes, his presence reinforces the impression that television shapes the thoughts and desires of people today and tomorrow. Sounding much like a reactionary interviewer in the David Frost mold, he babbles in an inane, obsequious manner, often stating the obvious or setting himself up as the spokesman for millions of television viewers.

The Carlssons' television set remains turned on throughout the entire teleplay, and Watkins uses these additional sounds and images in various ways. Occasionally, as when State Secretary Andersson speaks, the television becomes the center of attention. More often it is used to complement or to counterpoint events taking place in the apartment. For example, during the tense meal, scenes from Walt Disney's *Alice in Wonderland* serve as a metaphor for Bertil and Bo's sojourn in this strange underground world. Most significantly, however, the numerous television news programs present fragments from contemporary life in the year 2000 and a capsule world history of the last thirty years of the twentieth century. The differences among the newscasters exist only in terms of style and nationalistic nuances; their messages are all strikingly similar. On the one hand, they emphasize a constant state of danger which exists because of terrorist attacks by "antisocial elements." They admit that conditions have been difficult in the past, but, on the other hand, they all suggest that through discipline, striving, self-sacrifice, and tight military control, "the standard of living is going to rise unwaveringly in the future." As such, these news commentators act as a type of chorus to support the Fascist arguments posed by John in his debate with Bertil. The grim humor of the teleplay exists in the satiric portrayal of the news commentators. Especially memorable are the Frenchman, who eats the traditional dessert "Coupe Serreur" on camera, and the two Americans, Ron and Dave, who could have served as prototypes for Earl Camenbert and Floyd Robertson, the silly newscasters satirized on the *Second City* television show.

Finally, as in many of his films, Watkins establishes a structure in *The Trap* which suggests that what is seen are actually "real events" being filmed by an on-the-spot television crew for some specific television production. Watkins, however, uses newsreel images of starving African children and police arrests of "antisocial elements" which are neither part of this simulated television production nor part of the material shown on the television news programs. As in his previous work, he inserts this footage to break down the illusion that he has so carefully set up in order to subvert traditional form, but the detachment from the drama depicted often paradoxically involves the viewer even more. In the case of *The Trap*, these images support the ideas of Bertil. In one sense, they are images of conscience which the viewer must consider in choosing between the alternatives posed in the film.

Over the years, Watkins has come to believe with increasing conviction that the media of television and film have created "a response-orientated society." Each year he reconsiders his position as a filmmaker and wonders whether he should stop making films and "relate to people in smaller groups, face to face." Given this attitude, it is clear that the process of making a film or videoplay, like *The Trap*, with its intense communal participation, is as important to Watkins, if not more so, than the end result—the film or videoplay itself.

After the completion of *The Trap*, Watkins and Bo Melander made a preliminary outline for a teleplay tentatively called *The Nuclear Project* to be coproduced by Danmarks Radio and West German television. This teleplay was to carry on all of the techniques (handling of the cameras, multiple layers of sound, indirect studio lighting effects, and the use of nonprofessional actors) employed in *The Trap*. The outline described the activities of a hastily called conference in Hamburg after a major accident at the Indian Point nuclear power station in Westchester County, New York. Members of the United Nations International Atomic Energy Agency and representatives from most countries involved in the use of nuclear power come to this conference "in order to discuss and evaluate nuclear security and control safeguard standards." As in *The Trap*, Watkins and Melander wanted to use television news programs to show the activities of the outside world while the multiple factions at this meeting expressed their views. The pronuclear forces simply desire to reestablish the credibility of nuclear reactors by setting up better control standards. Delegates from the third world countries state that they will resist any attempt at international inspections in order to prevent any superpower from trying to control their development of nuclear technology. The antinuclear forces want to put all reactors out of production immediately. After various attempts at compromises, the emotional temperature of the delegates reaches the boiling point. Finally, a protesting antinuclear representative ("Though a majority is against atomic power, nobody listens to them. Freedom is dissolved.") is forcibly removed from the hall, and the conference degenerates into chaos.

The script treatment ends with the following paragraph:

Beyond the television monitor, we look at the many faces in the conference hall as the establishment tries rather vainly to restore order—the faces of the different delegates, the faces of the different environmentalists—some passionate—angry—crying—others embarrassed—stoic—indifferent—controlled—a few even amused. On this scene, we end the play. We do not know at this moment exactly what will be the final inference of the play, but a scene such as this seems the most appropriate way in which to end a vision of our near-future.

Apparently, executives from West German television did not think this an "appropriate way" to end the teleplay, or perhaps they were a bit nervous about the negative references in the outline to West Germany's plans to sell a uranium enriching plant to Brazil. In any event, they hastily withdrew from the project, and without their support, the Danes were forced to cancel the production.

Aftenlandet (Evening Land)

In October, 1975, at the invitation of Stig Björkman of the Danish Film Institute, Watkins began research on a feature film which was to be funded chiefly by the Institute and supported by two private producers, Steen Herdel and Ebbe Preisler. From the beginning of the project, tentatively called *Coup d'Etat*, Watkins worked closely with two Danish television writers, Poul Martinsen and Carsten Clante. Together they researched aspects of the Danish political scene in order to determine how a series of current problems (unemployment, growing defense ties among all European Common Market countries, terrorist kidnappings, and nation-wide strikes) might affect the "model" social democracy of Denmark. At first, Watkins envisioned the climax of his film in terms of a military takeover by right-wing elements, but that was deemed somewhat unrealistic given the low-profile position of the armed forces in Danish society. Therefore, for five months Watkins worked with his scriptwriters in trying to create the basis for a realistic, political film firmly rooted in present-day events. The unconventional script they developed closely paralleled all of Watkins' scripts since *Punishment Park*. There were extensive pages of research notes, a brief outline, and almost no written dialogue.

After placing notices in Copenhagen newspapers, Watkins assembled a cast of 192 nonprofessional actors and began shooting in March of 1976. In almost all cases, the participants expressed their own opinions and / or improvised their own dialogue. In the few cases where improvisation was ineffective, Poul Martinsen simply wrote out lines of dialogue on the spot. The cast was generally cooperative, and Watkins even managed to get Joan Churchill (who shot *Punishment Park*) to be his camerawoman. Yet the shooting of this particular film was perhaps the most harrowing of his career.

In 1966, the Danish police provided complete cooperation and assistance to Alfred Hitchcock when he shot sequences of *Torn Curtain* in Copenhagen. Ten years later, they were not about to extend the same courtesy to Peter Watkins and his crew. Weeks after Watkins requested aid from the police in shooting some of the film in the city's streets, a letter was sent by the Copenhagen chief of police indicating that he could be of no assistance because Watkins' film was a political film. The police chief, of course, had no right to make this kind of evaluation, and after complaints were made to higher authorities, the Danish minister of justice wrote a letter indicating that the police would cooperate "when possible" for them to do so. During much of the filming, however, the police obstructed the production "when possible" for them to do so. They refused to allow the use of any of their police uniforms and police cars for the production, and they frequently stopped, to the point of harrassment, technicians driving the makeshift police cars used in the film, even though all of the decals were covered over when scenes were not being shot. The police also refused, on a number of occasions, to grant the necessary permits for shooting the demonstration sequences, and they made obtaining permits for the use of fireworks and blanks a bureaucratic nightmare to rival episodes from Kafka's novels.[13]

Finally, after numerous delays and a serious problem with finance in the last stages of filming, Watkins finished the production stage and began the six-month task of editing the enormous amount of footage that had been shot. Fortunately, he was again assisted by Jeff McBride, who had worked with him on the editing of *The 70s People*. Soon after the editing began, Watkins changed the film's title from *Coup d'Etat* to

Evening Land, an allusion to a bleak quotation from the German philosopher Oswald Spengler.

The film is a chronologically structured work which begins with the strike of some 3,000 workers at an important civilian shipyard in Copenhagen. The workers are protesting an order for the building of four submarines to be supplied to the French. The order was secured by the financially troubled management which has also proposed to the workers that all pay increases be kept at four percent while work on the contract is being completed. In discussing the strike with a television interviewer, Sten Grønbech, director of the shipyard, admits that the submarines can be fitted with nuclear rockets, but he refuses to accept any responsibility for how "the customer uses the products."

At the same time, a summit meeting of European Common Market defense ministers is about to begin in Copenhagen, and although this meeting was scheduled months before, the striking workers, now arguing that "Denmark is not going to supply arms to the EEC army," look at the meeting as a direct provocation by the Danish Social Democrat government. Soon after the conference begins, a group of terrorists kidnap Jørgen Falck, the Danish market minister, and release a number of demands, which include an immediate stop to the production of nuclear submarines in Denmark, the immediate cessation of the EEC meeting, the holding of a new referendum on Denmark's membership in the EEC, and fulfillment of the strikers' demands.

The media and police immediately assume a connection between the terroists and the strikers and present this theory to the public as fact. The police also use the opportunity of the massive search for the kidnapped minister to conduct a series of raids against left-wing organizations and newspapers. The terrorists retaliate by threatening to blow up key targets in Copenhagen. Pressure to resign is placed on the Labor prime minister by the opposition party, and the Danish Federation of Unions finally decides to collaborate with government officials and to blacklist fifty of the strike leaders. When members of the strike committee discover this devious arrangement, they plan a massive march on the parliament buildings. Their demonstration, however, is brutally broken up by the police, and hundreds of workers are arrested. By this time the police have also located where Minister Falck is being held, and in a surprise raid, they rescue him and capture or kill the entire group of terrorists.

The film ends with discussions among members of the strike committee as to whether or not the strike will "peter out." The strikers now see themselves as victims of the authorities and the media in what they perceive to be the beginning stages of a police state. As such, for some members of the committee, the strike demands are intimately linked to human rights. "It's not just a question of politics. All this. It's really more to do with people and human rights. That's what it is. Shall our children grow up in a police state like this one here?" Although the strikers exhibit this concern, the film ends without suggesting how they will be able to develop and sustain a general strike.

Evening Land opened on February 18, 1977, in Copenhagen and four other Danish cities, as well as in Stockholm. Needless to say, the reaction of most Scandinavian critics was one of hostility. The film was attacked primarily for "lacking a political base." The Marxists expressed their dislike because

Watkins surveys amateur actors who will portray Danish policemen in *Evening Land.*

the film failed to show a direct line of action to be taken by the workers and because more sympathy was supposedly given to the terrorists than to the workers. Critics from more politically conservative newspapers echoed the tone of one reviewer who simply queried, "when will Peter Watkins learn to stop frightening the public?"[14]

Evening Land, Watkins' most political film since *Punishment Park*, avoids any kind of metaphorical frame and, instead, deals directly with problems current in Western Europe. The events depicted in the film are not merely possibilities for the near future; variations of them were occurring while the film was being made and shortly after it was released. The kidnapping and murder of West German industrialist Hanns-Martin Schleyer and former Italian Premier Aldo Moro by radical terrorists, the growing recession, unemployment, and strikes throughout Europe, and the international police coordination against terrorist activities should have reinforced the credibility and perhaps even probability of the vision of the near future presented in the film. Also, a mere two months after the release of *Evening Land*, photographs which might easily have been mistaken for stills from Watkins' film appeared in the April 26, 1977, issue of the Danish newspaper *Politken*. These photographs showed Danish police in full gear breaking up a demonstration at *Det Berlingske Hus*.

Those familiar with Watkins' Scandinavian films might at first perceive *Evening Land* as a step backward in his cinematic development. Gone, for instance, are the complex soundtrack overlays, the careful manipulation of silences, and a multilayer method of psychological investigation. It might be more appropriate, however, to consider the film as a step to the side—a parallel development of his style. In fact, Watkins stresses that he deliberately attempted to break away from what he achieved in *Edvard Munch* in order to establish, in *Evening Land*, a structure of confrontation chiefly through dialogue. The emphasis is also on directness, and thus Watkins, for the first time in his professional career, avoids the use of an off-screen narrator or a television interviewer who becomes a major character in the film. Although stylistically different from much of his other work, one of the purposes of *Evening Land* remains the same. Watkins again attempts to force his audience to reevaluate film and television structures by extending them beyond their conventional, present-day "response-oriented" uses. Also, in this film, especially through the use of Martin, the journalist who loses his job as industrial correspondent, Watkins tries to alert his audience to the dangers of the misuse of media in today's world.

The great achievement of *Evening Land* rests with the dialectic patterns that Watkins evolves through his editing. Though the film gives a "multifaceted newsreel" impression, its structure is meticulously controlled through the editing. Watkins' dialectical organization is especially complex because it is sustained throughout the entire film, and even if one employs Sergei Eisenstein's A + B = C shot structure to analyze the editing process, the constantly shifting nuances in each term of the equation alter the meanings of the terms even within the same shot. As such, generalizations become almost impossible. The strike committee, for example, does not represent a consistent position at any one time. It is made up of numerous views which are continuously changing, and thus the terms of the dialectic shift every time a new juxtaposition is posed. These permutations multiply throughout the film, and as such, its very structure comes to reflect the difficulties of coming to understand the pressures and implications of events which affect us today. Of course, the film does not propose any kind of dogmatic solution. Watkins wants his viewers to try to understand and to evaluate the situations he depicts. Perhaps then the audience will discuss, not the film, but these situations, and will arrive at decisions through an increased awareness. This is Watkins' greatest hope, and his belief in the integrity of his audience stands as the cornerstone of his methods of filmmaking.

Although his film is structured entirely in dialectical terms, Watkins claims "there is an underlying motif of anxiety and passion for the state of our entire system—and the total purpose of *Evening Land* is summed up by its plea at the conclusion for a greater awareness of the *human* dilemmas facing our society."[15] The problem with this statement is that Maj Britt's dialogue at the end of the film (already quoted in the plot summary) is probably not strong enough to support this claim. Poul Martinsen has indicated that he and Watkins conceived a slightly different ending which exhibited a new strength among many of the workers as they discussed how to change their tactics. Perhaps in this context, the emphasis on "the *human* dilemmas" would have been greater. A single take of such a sequence was shot, but it did not turn out very well, and unfortunately, financial problems did not allow for this material to be refilmed.

Evening Land is a difficult film in part because so much information is presented in dialogue form by a multitude of characters who exist primarily as mouthpieces for political, social, and economic positions. As such, the film never really grips the viewer in the same manner as most of Watkins' other works. The film's major flaw, however, concerns the depiction of the terrorists. Watkins maintains that terrorists throughout the world are being blamed for the unrest in our society, when the real causes are to be found in "the economic and spiritual climate" of our culture: "Under no circumstances would I justify murder or kidnapping, but at the same time I think it is necessary to balance the violence of the 'terrorists' against the violence within our system—as evinced, for example, by the escalating arms race—and that *balance* is the essential purpose of making *Evening Land*, and the essential thread that runs through the structure of the film."[16]

In attempting to establish this balance, Watkins slips into a somewhat unrealistic, even romanticized, portrait of the terrorist group. The terrorists call themselves "nonviolent," and perhaps to further this illusion, Watkins does not show the actual kidnapping of Minister Falck. Also, the terrorists, whose faces are never shown in the film, were portrayed by members of an underground theater group, and unfortunately their improvised dialogue degenerates to the level of clichéd rhetoric, at exactly the moments where it should not have done so.

Although it could have been a much stronger film had Watkins made the terrorists as ruthless as members of the Red Brigade, *Evening Land* remains practically the only serious political film about life in Western society in the late 1970s. While this fact seems to have eluded the Scandinavian critics, it was duly acknowledged in France, where the film was recognized as a major political work which "can develop analysis and true thinking" in the viewer.[17] Most French critics went on to praise the film's technical accomplishments and its brilliant dialectic structure. At about the same time these reviews were being published, however, Ole Espersen, chairman of the *Programudvalget* (Danmarks Radio's board of governors), wrote Watkins a letter. Incredible as it may sound to anyone who has endured a typical evening of Danish television, Espersen refused to telecast *Evening Land* because it did not, "in our opinion, in its form reach a standard which DR finds necessary."[18]

Given responses such as this one and the overall attitudes of television and film executives in Norway, Denmark, and Sweden to his work, it should not be difficult to understand why Watkins finally deemed it necessary to leave Scandinavia and to begin what would amount to another period of self-exile in his life.

6

Postscript: Prospects for the Future

IN EARLY 1977, West German television proposed that Watkins make a film biography of the Russian composer Alexander Scriabin. This proposal was quickly followed by an offer from RAI (Italtelevisionfilm) to produce a film on the futurist poet Filippo Tommaso Marinetti. Watkins decided to accept both projects because, along with his already completed *Edvard Munch*, these films would form a "trilogy on modernism." His work plan for these two films was unique; each would be thoroughly researched and shot, and then he would spend up to eighteen months editing both films which would be released simultaneously. Unfortunately, a change in the administrative executives at the West German channel which proposed the Scriabin film brought about the collapse of the project. Plans for the Marinetti film have also ground to a halt as a consequence of the German cancellation, the hopelessly bureaucratic structure at RAI, and Italy's unstable economic situation. At this point in time, it is questionable if this film will ever be made.

This situation is especially regrettable since Watkins had secured the complete cooperation of Marinetti's daughter and had even loosely blocked out the film's structure and his approach to this controversial figure. For Watkins, the key to Marinetti rests with the contradictions in his life and character:

> . . . a man full of bravura who was at the same time very insecure—a man who launched a movement despising romanticism who was probably one of the most incurable romantics in all Italy—a man who launched a movement attacking the role of women (though this is complex) who was himself constantly occupied with them—both superficially (at first) and then increasingly deeply. Behind these and

189

many other personal contradictions can probably be found many of
the contradictions inherent in Futurism itself—providing both its
strength and also the reason for its ultimate collapse.[1]

With the postponement of the film on Marinetti, Watkins
found himself in a rather difficult financial situation, but he
decided against pursuing offers for other television productions. Instead, in the fall of 1978, he decided to undertake a
minimally funded, three-month media research project in Australia, in order to create the Peoples' Commission, a committee of citizens dedicated to studying the role of media in today's world. The reason for this impractical decision is not
especially difficult to understand. Watkins is deeply concerned about the possible adverse physiological and
psychological effects of television and film on viewers, and
during the last ten years, he has frequently lectured at colleges
and universities throughout Europe, North America, and Australia, not so much to discuss his own work as to draw attention
to what he believes is a crisis in media.

In fact, Watkins' methods of filmmaking should be viewed
as evolving chiefly from his reactions against traditional media
structures. For him, "there is no such thing as truth in
media. . . . All media, all film is propaganda, corporate or personal, but it is propaganda. Controlled images and controlled
sounds."[2] In the early years of his career, he attempted to
counter the power of corporate propaganda by making "strong
personal propaganda films." He created complex filmic structures in reaction to the traditional sound-sync, chronological,
theatrical structure because he argued that the artificiality of
this form glosses over reality:

> It imposes a language system on us which is very much detracting
> from any kind of complex perception of the subject being dealt
> with. . . . We see something in sync in a ABCDEF structure, but the
> problem is that we don't perceive life in that way. This language sys-
> tem is totally antithetical to our way of perceiving. . . . Fifteen years
> ago, I was very consciously trying to work against those rhythms and
> to try and find other ways of dealing with sociological subjects and
> historical subjects.[3]

Although throughout the years Watkins' work has broken
away from the conformity of techniques which so often lull
and deaden viewing audiences, he now fears that his efforts

are not enough. He is afraid that in the present situation even his work contributes to a system that allows no return dialogue and thus encourages "withdrawal from participation." His present criticism of media calls all into doubt—even his own work. "I don't think that it's possible to discuss these things and be a filmmaker or television program maker at the same time. That's the problem."[4] Watkins' agony over this issue is genuine, and thus there is a real question as to whether he will continue to make films and for how long.

Even if Peter Watkins decides not to make any more films, hopefully, in the near future, his rightful place in the history of contemporary film will finally be acknowledged. At present, Watkins still remains very much the outsider whose work is either viciously attacked ("offensive," "obsessive," "amateurish," "hysterical," and "paranoid") or simply ignored. Books on documentary often reduce him to a footnote, and critical surveys such as Ivan Butler's *Cinema in Britain*, Eric Rhode's *A History of the Cinema: From Its Origins to 1970*, and Gerald Mast's *A Short History of the Movies* dismiss him altogether. David Thomson's recent *A Biographical Dictionary of Film* contains short critical essays on over 800 figures "most critical to the history of cinema."[5] Watkins is not included in this collection, but Paul Wendkos, director of the *Gidget* films, is.

While film journals abound in articles discussing Robert Altman's complex use of sound, next to nothing has been published in the major journals about Watkins' intricate sound montages or his other innovations and achievements: his experiments in fracturing narrative form, his advances in techniques of reconstruction, his imaginative uses of color and indirect lighting, his involvement of nonprofessional actors who express their own feelings and assist him in breaking down rigid script structures, his subversion of traditional documentary modes, and, most significantly, his attempt to transcend the usual relationships between the film and the viewing audience.

Even those critics, like Penelope Gilliatt and Arthur Knight, who perceive Watkins' work in a favorable light often tend to champion only one of his works rather than his methods of making films. Others, like Basil Wright (*The Long View*) and Roy Armes (*A Critical History of British Cinema*) recognize some of the significant aspects of Watkins' style and methods, but they incorrectly claim that "he has never really moved on from the formula he evolved for *Culloden* and perfected in *The War Game*."[6] Among the so-called established film critics, only Raymond Durgnat has thus far discussed the importance of Watkins' methods and accorded him an adequate place in film history: "Watkins is as crucial as John Grierson in the development of documentary."[7]

Peter Watkins, however, is much more than an innovative artist who has not been given the recognition he so richly deserves. A careful analysis of his film career can generate emotions of anger and inspiration. Reactions to his work and details of his experiences in England, the United States, Norway, Sweden, and Denmark stand as an indictment against those who control and restrict media, limit the growth of the committed artist, and ignore the viewing public's sensitivity, intelligence, and desire for meaningful involvement. The inspiration comes from Watkins himself, who serves as a model not only to the struggling artist, but to all of us. Despite his many difficulties, Watkins, like Edvard Munch, has remained true to his own vision, true to his belief in the value of self-expression, and true to his faith in the worth and dignity of the individual. V. S. Pritchett called George Orwell "the conscience of his generation," and perhaps it is fitting to end this study by pointing out that, in many ways, Peter Watkins is the conscience of our generation.

Notes and References

Chapter One

1. Unless otherwise indicated, all quotations from Watkins in this chapter are from a taped conversation recorded on August 14, 1977.
2. From a taped discussion with Watkins while he was reediting the cinema release version of *Edvard Munch*, July 30, 1975.
3. "Running, Jumping and Never Standing Still," *Movie Maker* 2 (June, 1967), 261.
4. Cited in David Levy, "Peter Watkins: In Conversation," *Montreal Star*, March 26, 1977 sect. D, p. 10.
5. "Running, Jumping and Never Standing Still," p. 262.
6. Information derived from discussions with Stan Mercer, unit manager for *The Forgotten Faces*, July 7, 1977.
7. Peter Watkins, "*Dust Fever*," *Amateur Cine World* 4, no. 1 (July 5, 1962), 15.
8. From a cassette recorded on October 11, 1977, and sent by Watkins to the author.

Chapter Two

1. Cited in Alan Rosenthal, *The New Documentary in Action: A Casebook in Film Making* (Berkeley, 1971), p. 153.
2. From an interview with Dick Bush recorded on September 27, 1977.
3. "Protest at 'Sadistic' *Culloden* TV Show," *Birmingham Evening Mail*, December 17, 1964.
4. "Peter Watkins: An Interview," *Film Society Review* 7, nos. 7-9 (1972), 81.
5. Peter Watkins, "*Punishment Park*," *American Cinematographer* 52, no. 8 (August, 1971), 778.
6. "Peter Watkins: Cameraman at World's End," *Journal of Popular Film* 2, no. 3 (Summer, 1973), 233-34.

7. Cited in Tony Rose, "Faces of the '45," *Amateur Cine World* 8 (December 17, 1964), 835.

8. Ibid.

9. Ibid.

10. Cited in Rosenthal, p. 159.

11. Cited in Rose, *Movie Maker*, p. 263.

12. Cited in Rosenthal, p. 156.

13. James Blue and Michael Gill, "Peter Watkins Discusses His Suppressed Nuclear Film *The War Game*," *Film Comment* 3, no. 4 (Fall, 1965), 18-19.

14. From a taped discussion with Peter Watkins, June 27, 1978.

15. Rosenthal, p. 160.

16. Ibid., p. 159.

17. From a taped interview with Richard Cawston, July 7, 1977. Unless otherwise noted, material related to the BBC position on *The War Game* comes from this interview.

18. Blue and Gill, p. 14.

19. Cited in Bert Baker, "Depressing—Maybe; Horrific? No," *London Daily Worker*, February 1, 1966, p. 2.

20. From a taped discussion with Peter Watkins, April 12, 1973.

21. Sections of this letter are reprinted in Alan C. Coman, *"The War Game*: That Old Documentary Bugaboo," in *The Uses of Film in the Teaching of English* (Toronto, 1971), pp. 151-60.

22. "The Censorship Game," *London Sunday Mirror*, February 13, 1966, p. 17.

23. Cited by Watkins in the April 12, 1973 discussion.

24. From Kenneth Adam's letter to the author, dated April 14, 1977.

25. *Principles and Practice in Documentary Programmes* (London, 1972), pp. 24, 27.

26. From the Watkins interview of June 27, 1978. This particular section of the interview deals with the filmmaker's response to Coman's article.

27. Ibid.

28. William Lowther, "The Gathering Storm," *Macleans* 91, no. 11 (May 29, 1978), 23.

Chapter Three

1. From the taped interview with Watkins on August 14, 1977.

2. Raymond Durgnat, "The Great British Phantasmagoria," *Film Comment* 13, no. 3 (May-June 1977), 50.

3. Michael Vestey, "Explosion in the Pop World—and Jean's Debut," *London Look*, April 29, 1967, p. 30.

4. *Hollywood, England: The British Film Industry in the Sixties* (New York, 1974), p. 350.

5. "The Britain of Tomorrow?" *London Observer*, April 30, 1967.

6. From a taped discussion with Watkins on June 27, 1978. Unless otherwise noted all of Watkins' comments about *Privilege* are from this source.

7. *The Rebel* (New York, 1954), p. 21.

8. In the summer of 1972, Jay Kantor, Brando, and Watkins became involved in another Indian project, but it appears that the proposed film was deemed "too radical" by the Chicago clothing manufacturer who was to supply most of the financial backing.

9. Nicholas Gosling, from a taped interview with the author, June 28, 1977.

10. Information was derived from the author's interview with Peter Suschitzky, June 29, 1977.

11. Peter Watkins, from a cassette interview with the author, September 10, 1978.

12. "TV's Young Turks: Part Two," *Films and Filming*, 15, no. 7 (April, 1969), 27. Kevin Mcgee in an unpublished essay, "*Edvard Munch* and Brecht's Ideas on Epic Theatre," also makes a number of perceptive observations about the success of Watkins' detachment effects.

13. "Left, Right and Wrong: An Interview with Peter Watkins," *Films and Filming*, 16, no. 6 (March 1970), 28.

14. "*The Gladiators*: Film in Light of Current Events," *Dagens Nyheter*, June 26, 1969.

15. Watkins' interview of August 14, 1977.

16. Unless otherwise noted, background information has been obtained from Watkins' article in *American Cinematographer*.

17. Jim Pines, "The Orgasm in Its Bleakest Form: Peter Watkins on *Punishment Park*," *Time Out*, February 4-10, 1972, p. 42.

18. Peter Watkins, "An Open Letter to the Press," Oslo, January, 1972 (unpublished).

19. Cited in Pines, p. 43.

20. The interview appears in *Film and History* 8, no. 1 (February, 1977), 6-13, MacDonald's essay was read at the Third Purdue Conference on Film, April 28, 1978.

21. See Jean-Claude Bouis, "He Makes the Blood Spurt–Carefully," *Detroit Free Press*, May 9, 1978, sect. D, p. 7, and Gerald R. Barrett, "William Friedkin Interview," *Literature / Film Quarterly* 3 (Fall, 1975), 334-62.

22. John J. O'Connor, "Playing Fast and Loose with Recent History," *New York Times*, October 9, 1977, sect. 2, p. 39.

23. *Film Form* (New York, 1949), p. 84.

24. "*Punishment Park* and Dissent in the West," *Literature / Film Quarterly* 4 (Fall, 1976), 296.

25. From an open discussion with Watkins at Utica College, Utica,

New York, in March, 1975 (tape recorded).

26. *"Punishment Park* and Dissent in the West," p. 293. *Punishment Park* opened in London, in February 1972, to mixed reviews, and in November, 1973, it finally reached Paris where it was reasonably well received.

27. Cited in Pines, p. 43.

Chapter Four

1. Watkins, *"Edvard Munch:* A Director's Statement," *Literature / Film Quarterly* 5 (Winter, 1977), 18. Unless otherwise indicated, Watkins' quotations about *Edvard Munch* are taken from this essay.

2. Robert Philip Kolker poses a similar analysis of Russell's methods in "Ken Russell's Biopics: Grandier and Gaudier," *Film Comment* 9, no. 3 (May-June, 1973), 42-45.

3. Reinhold Heller, *Edvard Munch: The Scream* (London, 1973), p. 28.

4. (Oslo, 1972), p. 73.

5. Cited in Werner Timm, *The Graphic Art of Edvard Munch* (London, 1973), pp. 29-30.

6. Pål Hougen, interviewed by the author, August 15, 1975.

7. Tape recorded discussions with Watkins while he was reediting the cinema release version of the film, August 4-9, 1975.-

8. Cited in Oswald Doughty, *Dante Gabriel Rossetti: A Victorian Romantic* (New Haven, 1949), p. 5.

9. Discussions with Watkins, August 4-9, 1975.

10. Heller, p. 52.

11. Discussions with Watkins, August 4-9, 1975.

12. Ibid.

13. Laura R. Oswald, "Film Center," program notes for the School of the Art Institute of Chicago's screenings of *Edvard Munch*, February 9-15, 1978.

14. Discussions with Watkins, August 4-9, 1975.

15. Ibid.

16. Cited in Timm, p. 48.

17. Discussions with Watkins, August 4-9, 1975.

18. Ibid.

19. Odd Geir Saether, interviewed by the author in Oslo, August 14, 1975.

20. Cited in Heller, p. 49.

21. Saether interview.

22. From the text of a letter sent by Watkins to NRK in March, 1974.

23. Riktor's letter to Watkins, dated May 6, 1976.

24. From Watkins' letter to the author, dated December 6, 1975.

25. Ibid.

Chapter Five

1. From *"The 70s People (70-talets människor),"* an essay that Watkins prepared for an internal Sveriges Radio information newsletter.

2. Ibid.

3. Ibid.

4. From the author's discussion with Watkins, tape recorded on July 31, 1975.

5. From a June 1977 radio broadcast in which Lense-Møller dicussed Watkins' Scandinavian films.

6. From the author's discussion with Jeff McBride, July 2, 1977.

7. Information from Bo Melander, from a taped telephone interview with the author, on September 18, 1975.

8. Ibid.

9. From *"Fällan,"* an essay that Watkins wrote for the SR information newsletter. Unless otherwise noted, Watkins' comments on *The Trap* are from this essay.

10. From interviews conducted by the author with Paco Hårleman on August 7, 1975, and with Egon Blank on August 8, 1975.

11. Tore Breda Thoresen, in a letter to Watkins, dated August 28, 1978, and Bjørn Lense-Møller, in a letter to Watkins, dated August 11, 1978.

12. From the author's discussion with Watkins, tape recorded on August 4, 1975.

13. Information obtained from interviews conducted by the author with Jeff McBride on July 2, 1977, and with Poul Martinsen on July 4, 1977.

14. From reviews quoted in Watkins' unpublished "Statement to the Swedish Press."

15. From an unpublished essay written by Watkins on *Evening Land.* No title or date given.

16. Ibid.

17. Louis Marcorelles, *"Force de Frappe,* de Peter Watkins," *Le Monde,* March 31, 1978, p. 21.

18. Ole Espersen, in a letter to Watkins, dated June 13, 1978.

Chapter Six

1. From "F. T. Marinetti: Some Thoughts and Intentions," an unpublished essay written in Rome, in November, 1977.

2. From an unedited April 1978 interview with Watkins recorded by radio station KUOM.

3. Ibid.

4. From Watkins' lecture at Wayne State University, March 4, 1977.

5. (New York, 1976), p. viii.

6. Wright, *The Long View* (New York, 1974), p. 556.

7. "The Great British Phantasmagoria," *Film Comment* 13, no. 3 (May-June 1977), 50, and "Late Night Line Up," telecast on BBC-2 on August 16, 1971. It should also be pointed out that James M. Welsh, coeditor of *Literature / Film Quarterly*, has written frequently and intelligently about Watkins' work.

Selected Bibliography

Primary Sources

1. Books

The War Game. New York: Avon Books, 1967. An adaptation of *The War Game* script into book form.

2. Articles

"*Dust Fever.*" *Amateur Cine World* 4 (July 5, 1962), 12-18. This article offers a detailed plot summary of *Dust Fever*, a 75-minute film which unfortunately was never completed.

"*Edvard Munch*: A Director's Statement." *Literature / Film Quarterly* 5 (Winter, 1977), 17-22. This essay is crucial in attempting to understand *Edvard Munch* as a personal film.

"Peter Watkins Talks About the Suppression of His Work Within Britain." *Films and Filming* 17, no. 5 (February, 1971), 35-37. Watkins responds to Michael Armstrong's article on *The Gladiators*.

"*Punishment Park.*" *American Cinematographer* 52, no. 8 (August, 1971), 778-79. Watkins discusses the making of *Punishment Park*.

"*Punishment Park* and Dissent in the West." *Literature / Film Quarterly* 4 (Fall, 1976), 293-302. Watkins' essay was originally written in 1973 and covers the various ways in which *Punishment Park* was kept from being screened in the United States.

"Staging a Revolution." *Amateur Cine World* 4 (November 29, 1962), 804-5, 822. Watkins discusses the background of *The Forgotten Faces*, the preparation for filming, and the most memorable incidents during the nine-day shooting schedule.

3. Interviews

"Faces of the '45." *Amateur Cine World* 8 (December 17, 1964), 834-37. Tony Rose interviews Watkins about *Culloden* and the relationship between his amateur films and his first professional film.

"Left, Right and Wrong: An Interview with Peter Watkins." *Films and Filming* 16, no. 6 (March, 1970), 28-29. This interview focuses on *The Gladiators*.

199

"On the Making of *Edvard Munch*: Discussions with Peter Watkins
and Odd Geir Saether." *Film Criticism* 2, no. 1 (Fall, 1977),
36-42. Andrea and Joseph Gomez present statements by Watkins
on lighting, photography, editing, and involvement with actors.
Saether discusses technical problems encountered in the filming
of *Edvard Munch*.

"The Orgasm in Its Bleakest Form: Peter Watkins on *Punishment
Park*." *Time Out*, February 4-10, 1972, pp. 42-43. Jim Pines asks
perceptive questions about *Punishment Park*, and Watkins is
especially articulate in his responses.

"Peter Watkins: An Interview." *Film Society Review* 7, nos. 7-9
(1972), 72-84. Using *Punishment Park* as a point of departure, an
interviewer covers a variety of topics but focuses his questions
chiefly on political and social matters.

"Peter Watkins Discusses His Suppressed Nuclear Film *The War
Game*." *Film Comment* 3, no. 4 (Fall, 1965), 14-19. James Blue
and Michael Gill conducted this interview before the BBC decided to ban *The War Game*. Watkins describes his working
methods in detail.

"Peter Watkins: In Conversation." *Montreal Star*, March 26, 1977,
sect. D, p. 10. David Levy's interview is wide-ranging and important, especially when it touches on the subject of media.

"Peter Watkins: Therapeutic Cinema and the Repressive Mind."
Film and History 7, no. 1 (February, 1977), 6-13; 7, no. 2 (May,
1977), 34-42. James M. Welsh and Steven Philip Kramer talk with
Watkins after a particularly heated audience reaction to a 1974
screening of *Punishment Park* at Salisbury State College.

"*The War Game*: Peter Watkins." In *The New Documentary in Action*, ed. Alan Rosenthal; pp. 151-63. Berkeley: University of
California Press, 1971. Watkins discusses the background of the
film and his shooting methods.

Secondary Sources

1. Parts of Books

ARMES, ROY. *A Critical History of British Cinema*. New York: Oxford
University Press, 1978. In Chapter 17 ("An Art of the Real–Russell, Loach and Watkins"), Armes argues that "Watkins's concept
of the real is thus far richer than that of either Russell (who limits
himself to location work and authentically attested anecdote) or
Loach (who is bound by the need to create a perfect naturalistic
illusion of life). In Watkins's work there is a greater inner
dynamism, for reality implies life existing on both sides of the
camera, so that we are involved in the action and at the same time
aware that we are watching a film."

―――. *Film and Reality: An Historical Survey*. Harmondsworth,

Middlesex: Penguin Books, 1974. Chapter 10 ("Realist Film and Television Realism") deals with the films of Watkins and Ken Loach.

COMAN, ALAN C. *"The War Game*: That Old Documentary Bugaboo." In *The Uses of Film in the Teaching of English*. Curriculum Series no 8. Toronto: Ontario Institute for Studies in Education, 1971. Pp. 151-60. A long, sustained attack on *The War Game* as a piece of emotional propaganda. "This incredible rhetoric of film debate is matched by the verbal rhetoric, in an obvious travesty of the art of persuasion."

LEVIN, G. ROY. *Documentary Explorations*. Garden City, New York: Doubleday, 1971. The interview with Richard Cawston (pp. 73-94) contains a number of statements about Watkins' "subjective" films and a brief discussion about *The War Game* controversy.

MANVELL, ROGER. *New Cinema in Britain*. London: Studio Vista, 1969. Contains a brief but sympathetic discussion of Watkins' early films.

TYNAN, KENNETH. *"The War Game."* In *Tynan Right and Left: Plays, Films, People, Places and Events*. New York: Atheneum, 1968. Pp. 254-55. This is a reprint of Tynan's "A Warning Masterpiece" review from *The Observer*, including the statement that *The War Game* "may be the most important film ever made."

WALKER, ALEXANDER. *Hollywood England: The British Film Industry in The Sixties*. London: Michael Joseph, 1974. Pp. 343-51. Walker presents the background for the funding of *Privilege* and discusses why it was given limited exposure in England.

WELSH, JAMES M. "The Cinema of Intimacy: Peter Watkins's Portrait of the Artist as a Young Munch." In *Explorations in National Cinemas: The 1977 Film Studies Annual, Part One*, ed. Ben Lawton and Janet Staiger, pp. 74-91. Pleasantville, New York: Redgrave Publishing Co., 1977. A significant essay which rightly claims that *Edvard Munch* is "the most important film so far in the stormy career of Peter Watkins."

WRIGHT, BASIL. *The Long View*. New York: Alfred A. Knopf, 1974. Pp. 554-58. Wright presents a particularly sensitive analysis of *Punishment Park* in his discussion of Watkins' films: *"Punishment Park* is of course offensive—deliberately so. But the paranoia is not so much in Watkins as in the society in which he as a creative film-maker is living, and whose sickness he tries to signal before it is too late."

2. Articles

ANON. "Man's Right to Know Before He Dies." *Film Comment* 3, no. 4 (Fall, 1965), 2-13. A compilation of British press clippings related to *The War Game*.

ARMSTRONG, MICHAEL. "A Passionate Plea For Peter Watkins, Myself and You." *Films and Filming* 17, no. 1 (October, 1970), 46, 51-52. A long, complex review of *The Gladiators* which, although sympathetic, suggests that Watkins fails as an artist. The review ends with an emotional outburst that "we need people like Peter Watkins who should be provided with every opportunity to cry out in the name of Truth before it is too late for all of us."

CANBY, VINCENT. "Film Festival: Fascination With Effects of Horror." *New York Times*, October 12, 1971, p. 50. This review and one by Judith Crist probably caused Sherpix to drop the U.S. distribution of *Punishment Park*.

DURGNAT, RAYMOND. "The Great British Phantasmagoria." *Film Comment* 13, no. 3 (May-June, 1977), 48-53. "Perhaps Watkins is as crucial as John Grierson in the development of documentary."

_____. "TV's Young Turks: Part Two." *Films and Filming* 15, no. 7 (April, 1969), 26-30. Durgnat offers a perceptive analysis of *The War Game* and *Privilege*.

GILLMAN, PETER. "The War Film the BBC Won't Show." *London Sunday Times Magazine*, January 9, 1966, pp. 28-33. This article presents a summary of events leading to the BBC's decision to ban *The War Game*.

GOMEZ, JOSEPH A. "Peter Watkins's *Edvard Munch*." *Film Quarterly* 30, no. 2 (Winter, 1976-1977), 38-46. Much of the material contained in this essay has been incorporated into chapter 4 of this book.

KAWIN, BRUCE. "Peter Watkins: Cameraman at World's End." *Journal of Popular Film* 2 (Summer, 1973), 231-42. Kawin argues that all of Watkins' major films are about media. *Punishment Park* "clarifies a tension which is suddenly seen to run through Watkins' work as a whole: the problem of the inadequate or unreachable audience."

ROSE, TONY. "Running, Jumping and Never Standing Still." *Movie Maker* 2 (June, 1967), 260-63. Clearly the best single article on the amateur films of Peter Watkins.

RUSSELL, JOHN. "*Edvard Munch* – A Film Truer to Life Than to Art." *New York Times*, September 12, 1976, sect. 2, pp. 1, 33. "Peter Watkins's film on Munch is roomy . . . , beautiful to look at, and very good indeed in its presentation of Munch's childhood and youth."

SHAHEEN, JACK G. "*The War Game*." *Film Society Review* 7, nos. 7-9 (1972), 85-91. Shaheen's essay covers *The War Game* controversy. Unfortunately, no context is given for the quotations cited in the essay.

SIMON, JOHN. "Suffering Artist, Smiling Dictator." *New York*, September 13, 1976, pp. 89-91. Even though Simon thinks that *Edvard Munch* "is ultimately a failure," he claims that "it is the most magnificent failure" he has seen "in a good many years."

VAUGHN, SUSAN BEACH. "Death of a Filmmaker." *Arts in Society* 10 (1973), 293-95. This essay incorporates a number of quotations from Watkins' discussions at the 1972 Atlanta Film Festival. The focus is on media cutting off two-way communication.

VESTEY, MICHAEL. "Explosion in the Pop World—and Jean's Debut" *London Look*, April 29, 1967, pp. 28-33. A pop writer's behind-the-scenes look at *Privilege*.

WEINER, BERNARD. "*Punishment Park*." *Film Quarterly* 25, no. 4 (Summer, 1972), 49-52. A favorable review of the film. "*Punishment Park* is the most important contemporary film on the subject of the present and future of the American radical movement."

WELSH, JAMES M. "Cinematic Portraiture: Peter Watkins and Edvard Munch." *Washington Review of the Arts* 2, no. 4 (Winter, 1976-1977), 18-19. This review surveys the career of Peter Watkins and treats *Edvard Munch* as a film that is "incontestably biographical" but also autobiographical.

YOUNG, VERNON. "War Games: Work in Progress." *Hudson Review* 22, no. 1 (Spring, 1969), 128-33. Young's impressions of a Watkins press conference: "Rarely have I heard such a rush of ill-conceived and paranoid remarks."

3. Unpublished Material

MACDONALD, SCOTT. "Audience Reaction to *Punishment Park*." An essay read at the Third Purdue Conference on Film, April 28, 1978. Hopefully this excellent essay will be in print in the near future.

Filmography

1. *Amateur Films*

THE WEB(1956) 8mm
Rental: Institute of Amateur Cinematographers, 63 Woodfield Lane, Ashtead, Surrey, KT21 2BT, England

THE FIELD OF RED (1958) 16mm
(unavailable)

DIARY OF AN UNKNOWN SOLDIER(1959) 16mm
Script, Production, Direction, Camera, and Editing by Peter Watkins
Cast: Playcraft Film Unit
16mm rental: Institute of Amateur Cinematographers

THE FORGOTTEN FACES(1961) 16mm
Unit Managers: John Newing, Stan Mercer
Script: Peter Watkins
Cinematographer: Michael Hall
Assistant Cameraman: Peter Mills
Properties: Johnny Horne
Fire Arms: Roger Caltham
Make-up: Angela Williams
Catering: Phil Mercer
Editor: Peter Watkins
Narrator: Frank Hickey
Cast: Michael Roy, John Newing, Stan Mercer, Irene Mallaid, John Lawrence, Alan Pope, Angela Williams, Eve Hopper, Roger Coltham, Nick Evans, Geraldine Roy, Joan Tilke, Frances Mercer, Irene Cooper, Roy Todd, Andria Duncan, Carol Heslop, Michael Chester, Steve Mercer, Barry Campbell, Johnny Horne, Michael

Rutledge, Alfred Mallaid, Brian Turner, Roger Day, Geoff Sanders, Andrew Thatcher, Brian Ashby
16mm Rental: Institute of Amateur Cinematographers

DUST FEVER(1962), never finished.

2. *Professional Films*
CULLODEN(BBC, 1964)
Production Unit: Valerie Booth, Geoff Sanders, Rodney Barnes, Roger Higham, Michael Powell, Jennifer Howie, Geraldine Proudfoot
Script: Peter Watkins
Cinematographer: Dick Bush
Design: Ann Davey, Brendon Woods, Colin MacLeod, John Shaw
Make-up: Ann Brodie
Battle Co-ordinator: Derek Ware
Historical Adviser: John Prebble
Music: "My Bonnie Moorhen" sung by Colin Cater
Sound: John Gatland, Lou Hanks
Editor: Michael Bradsell
Running Time: 75 minutes
16mm Rental: Time-Life Films

THE WAR GAME(BBC, 1966)
Production Assistant: Peter Norton
Script: Peter Watkins
Cinematographer: Peter Bartlett
Make-up: Lilias Munro
Costumes: Vanessa Clarke
Action Sequences: Derek Ware
Design: Tony Cornell, Anne Davey
Sound: Derek Williams, Lou Hanks, Stanley Morcom
Editor: Michael Bradsell
Commentary: Dick Graham, Michael Aspel
Running Time: 47 minutes
16mm Rental: Images, 2 Purdy Ave., Rye, N. Y. 10580, and Films Inc.

PRIVILEGE(Universal, 1967)
Producer: John Heyman
Associate Producer: Timothy Burrill
Assistant Director: Scott Wodehouse

Script: Norman Bogner, from an original story by John Speight, with
    additional scenes and dialogue by Peter Watkins.
Cinematographer: Peter Suschitzky
Art Director: Bill Brodie
Action Sequences: Derek Ware
Costumes: Vanessa Clarke
Music: Mike Leander, songs by Mike Leander and Mark London
Sound: Ian Bruce
Editor: John Trumper
Cast: Paul Jones (Steven Shorter), Jean Shrimpton (Vanessa), Mark
    London (Alvin), William Job (Butler), Max Bacon (Uncle Julie),
    Jeremy Child (Crossley), James Cossins (Tatham), Frederick
    Danner (Hooper), Victor Henry (Freddie K), Arthur Pentelow
    (Stanley), Steve Kirby (Squit), Michael Barrington (Bishop of Es-
    sex), Edwin Fink (Bishop of Cornwall), John Gill (Bishop of Sur-
    rey), Norman Pitt (Bishop of Hersham), Alba (Bishop of Rutland),
    Malcolm Rogers (Rev. Tate), Doreen Mantle (Miss Crawford),
    Michael Graham (TV Director)
Running Time: 103 minutes
16mm Rental: Twyman Films, 329 Salem Ave. Dayton, Ohio 45401;
    Universal 16, 445 Park Ave., New York, N. Y. 10022

GLADIATORERNA (THE GLADIATORS British title, **THE
    PEACE GAME)** (A Sandrews Film, 1969)
Executive Producer: Bo Jonsson
Producer: Goran Lindgren
Script: Peter Watkins, Nicholas Gosling
Cinematographer: Peter Suschitzky
Art Director: William Brodie
Costumes: Chris Collins
Music: Claes of Geijerstam, Gustav Mahler (Third Symphony)
Sound: Tage Sjoborg
Special Effects: Stig Lindberg
Editor: Lars Hagström
Cast: Keith Bradfield (Narrator), Richard Friday (B-4), Pik-Sen Lim
    (C-2), Jean-Pierre Delamour (B-3), Arthur Pentelow (British
    General), Frederick Danner (British Staff Officer), Kenneth Lo
    (Chinese Colonel), Bjorn Franzen (Swedish Colonel), Hans
    Bendrik (Captain Davidsson), Tim Yum (Chinese Staff Officer),
    Daniel Harle (French Officer), Hans Berger (West German Of-
    ficer), Jurgen Schling (East German Officer), Rosario Gianetti
    (American Officer), Stefan Dillan (Russian Officer), Ugo Chiari
    (Italian Officer), Chandrakant Desai (Indian Officer), George
    Harris (Nigerian Officer), Christer Gynge (Assistant Controller),

Jeremy Child (B-1), Erich Sterling (B-2), Roy Scammell (B-5), J. Z. Kennedy (B-6), Eberhard Fehmers (B-7), Terry Whitmore (B-8), Nguyen (B-9), To Van Minh (B-10)
Running Time: 105 minutes
16mm Rental: New Line Cinema, 853 Broadway, New York, N. Y. 10023

PUNISHMENT PARK(A Chartwell Films-François Films Production, 1971)
Producer: Susan Martin
Assistant Director: Peter Smokler
Script: Peter Watkins, with the cooperation of cast members who often improvised their dialogue.
Cinematographer: Joan Churchill
Art Director: David Hancock
Music: Paul Motian
Sound: Mike Moore
Sound Mixing: Hiroki Yamoto, Wayne Nakatsu
Editor: Peter Watkins and Terry Hodel
Cast: Mark Keats (Chairman Hoeger), Kent Foreman (Lee Robert Brown), Carmen Argenziano (Jay Kaufman), Cathrine Quittner (Nancy Jane Smith), Scott Turner (Defendant Kohler), Mary Ellen Kleinhall (Allison Mitchner), Luke Johnson (Luke Valerio), Stan Armstead (Charles Robbins), Frederick Franklyn (Defense Attorney), Gladys Golden, Sanford Golden, George Gregory, Norman Sinclair, Sigmund Rich, Paul Rosenstein (Tribunal Members), Joe Hudgins (Chief Tribunal Marshal), Gary Johnson, Michele Johnson, Ted Martin, Don McDonald, Harold Schneider (Pacifist Defendants in the Desert), Roland Gonzalez, Viola Gonzalez, Jack Gozdick, Brian Hart, Linda Mandel, Don Pino, Jason Sommers, Conchita Thornton (Semi-militant Defendants in the Desert), Harold Beaulieu, Cynthia Jenkins, Jack London, Rob Lewine (Militant Defendants in the Desert), Lee Marks (FBI Agent Donovan), Jim Bowan (Captain Edwards), Paul Alelyunes, Kerry Cannon, Bob Franklin, Bruce McGuire, Ron Pennington, Allen Powell, Jim Wettstein (City Police), Jim Churchill, Danny Conlon, Wally McKay, Don Vann, Charlie Wyatt (National Guard)
Running Time: 88 minutes
16mm Rental: Videotape Network, 115 E. 62 Street, New York, N. Y. 10021 (also available in videotape format)

EDVARD MUNCH(A Norsk Rikskringkasting / Sveriges Radio AB Production, 1974)
Production Manager: Ulf Fjoran

Script: Peter Watkins, with additional dialogue by cast members
Cinematographer: Odd Geir Saether
Art Director: Grethe Hejer
Costumes: Ada Skolmen
Make-up: Karin Saether
Sound: Kenneth Storm-Hansen, Bjorn Hansen
Lighting: Erik Daeli, Cato Bautz, Willy Bettvik
Research: Anne Veflingstad
Artistic Advisers: Knut Jorgensen, Hermann Bendiksen
Dialogue Adviser: Ase Vikene
Editor: Peter Watkins, with the assistance of Lorne Morris
Cast: Geir Westby (Edvard Munch), Gro Fraas (Mrs. Heiberg), Kjersti
　　Allum (Sophie in 1868), Erik Allum (Edvard in 1868), Susan
　　Troldmyr (Laura in 1868), Ragnvald Caspari (Peter Andreas in
　　1868), Katja Pedersen (Inger in 1868), Hjørdis Ulriksen (House-
　　maid), Inger-Berit Oland (Sophie in 1875), Åmund Berge (Ed-
　　vard in 1875), Camilla Falk (Laura in 1875), Erik Kristiansen (Pe-
　　ter Andreas in 1875), Anne-Marie Daehli (Inger in 1875), Johan
　　Halsbog (Dr. Christian Munch), Gro Jarto (Laura Cathrine
　　Munch), Berit Rytter Hasle (Laura Munch as an adult), Lotte
　　Teig (Aunt Karen Bjolstad), Rachel Pedersen (Inger Munch as an
　　adult), Gunnar Skjetne (Peter Andreas Munch as an adult),
　　Vigdis Nilssen (Housemaid), Eli Ryg (Oda Lasson), Knut Khris-
　　tiansen (Christian Krohg), Nils-Eger Pettersen (Fritz Thaulow),
　　Morten Eid (Sigbjørn Obstfelder), Haakon Gundersen (Vilhelm
　　Krag), Peter Esdaile (Dr. Thaulow), Dag Myklebust (Sigurd
　　Bodtker), Kristen Helle-Valle (Miss Drefsen), Torstein Hilt
　　(Jappe Nilssen), Ida Elisabeth Dypvik (Åse Carlsen), Ellen
　　Waaler (Charlotte Dornberger), Kåre Stormark (Hans Jaeger),
　　Alf-Kåre Strindberg (August Strindberg), Iselin von Hanne Bast
　　(Dagny Juell), Ladislaw Reznicek (Stanislaw Przybyszewski),
　　Christer Fredberg (Adolf Paul), Kai Olshausen (Dr. Schlittgen),
　　Dieter Kriszat (Richard Dehmel), Peter Saul (Ola Hansson),
　　Merete Jorgenssen (Laura Marholm), Einar Henning Smedby
　　(Pianist)
Running Time: Television version–210 minutes; Cinema release
　　version–167 minutes
Premier: Cinema release version–New York, September 12, 1976
16mm Rental: New Yorker Films, 43 West 61st Street, New York, N. Y.
　　10023

70-TALETS MÄNNISKOR (THE 70S PEOPLE)(Danmarks Radio,
　　1975)
Production Department: Palle Wolfsberg, Kristen Christensen, Inge
　　Wolle, Ole Guldbranden

Script: Peter Watkins, in cooperation with cast members who expressed their own feelings and ideas
Cinematographer: Henrik Herbert
Art Director: Leif Hedager
Music: Music and lyrics from "The Jolson Story"
Sound: Andreas Møller
Sound Mixing: Troels Orland, Henrik Carlsen
Editor: Peter Watkins, with the assistance of Jeff McBride
Cast: Jette Jørgensen (Kathrine), Inge Lundgren (Mother), Erik L. Christensen (Fleming), Anne Kathrine Holm (Anne), Elisabeth Hastrup (Mother), Frederick Rils-Petersen (Father), Christian Rosenstand Koux (Brother), Margit Carolsfeld-Krause (Grandmother), Susanne Andreassen (Girl in Skyscraper), Kristen Jorgensen (Mother), Jørgen Vierø (Father), Randi Jensen (Patient in Hospital)
Reconstructed Interviews: Niels-Anker Hansen, Tom Hayem, Anders Steensen Bille, Per Krarup, Hildur Jackson, John K. Olsen, Henrik Johansen, Lis Anja Petersen, and the citizens of Christiania
Consultative Assistance and Cast: Jens Guldbaek, Christian Lyhne, Kirsten Rudfeld, Karsten Jensen, Tine Bryld, Jørgen Wolfe, Johannes Lomholt
Running Time: 127 minutes
16mm Rental: Not available in the United States

FÄLLAN (THE TRAP)(Sveriges Radio-2, 1975)
Producer: Stig Palm
Production Assistant: Monika Barthelson
Script: Peter Watkins, Bo Melander, from an original idea by Bo Melander, with additional dialogue by cast members
Cameramen: Allen Mauritzon, Raymond Wemmenlöv, Bengt Ove Gustavsson, Torsten Törnquist, Lars Bermann
Technical Director: Egon Blank
Lighting: Paco Härleman
Costumes: Gunnel Nilsson
Sound: Rolf Berling
Cast: Karl Lennart Sandquist (John), Bo Melander (Bertil), Anita Kronevi (Margareta), Jonas Berg (Bo), Thomas Carlsson (Peter), Svetoslav Botchvarov, Jean Chapou, Axel Fritz, Gösta Gemne, Ronald Hoiseck, Davis Jones, Torsten Nilsson (TV commentators), Terry Whitmore, Charles Koroly, Larry Martin (American Guards), Hans Olofsson, Peter Lindkvist (Swedish Guards), Vatentin Agopov, Vladimir Margineanu, Viktor Pylypenko (Russian Guards), Dominique Amoloo, Arne Franzen, Georg Gough, Ronald Gustafson, Eunan Sheridan (Technicians), Hans Asph, Lars Falkeman Åke Karlsson, Bertil Kleine, Ingvar Storm (Tunnel Workers)

Running Time: 65 minutes
16mm Rental: Not available in the United States at this time, but
    plans for distribution in video cassette form are being considered

AFTENLANDET (EVENING LAND)(1980 Film / APS, 1977)
Producer: Ebbe Preisler, Jeff McBride, Steen Herdel
Supported by: The Danish Film Institute
Script: Carsten Clante, Poul Martensen, Peter Watkins, but the cast
    members also expressed their own opinions and feelings.
Cinematographer: Joan Churchill
Costumes: Gunnel Nilsson
Music: Anders Koppel
Editor: Peter Watkins, Jeff McBride
Cast: 192 nonprofessional actors
Running Time: 110 minutes
16mm Rental: New Yorker Films plans to distribute the film

Videotape-Slide Presentation: **STATE OF THE UNION** (Videotape
    Network, 1971)
Script and Narration: Peter Watkins
Running Time: 90 minutes
Videotape Rental: Videotape Network

Index